W9-AQE-722

John Rastell

Twayne's English Authors Series

Arthur F. Kinney, Editor
University of Massachusetts, Amherst

TEAS 363

PRINTER'S DEVICES USED BY JOHN RASTELL
Reproduced by permission of the British Library

John Rastell

By Albert J. Geritz
Fort Hays State University

and Amos Lee Laine
Hampden-Sydney College

Twayne Publishers • *Boston*

CARNEGIE LIBRARY
LIVINGSTONE COLLEGE
SALISBURY, N. C. 28144

John Rastell

Albert J. Geritz
Amos Lee Laine

Copyright © 1983 by G. K. Hall & Company
All Rights Reserved
Published by Twayne Publishers
A Division of G. K. Hall & Company
70 Lincoln Street
Boston, Massachusetts 02111

Book Production by Marne B. Sultz

Book Design by Barbara Anderson

Printed on permanent/durable acid-free
paper and bound in the United States of
America.

Library of Congress Cataloging in
Publication Data

Geritz, Albert J.
    John Rastell.

    (Twayne's English authors series; TEAS 363)
    Bibliography: p. 120
    Includes index.
    1. Rastell, John, d. 1536—Criticism and
interpretation.   I. Laine, Amos Lee.   II. Title.   III. Series.
PR2336.R4Z6   1983   001.3'092'4   83-270
ISBN 0-8057-6849-1

001.3
R229

For Laura, Suzanna, and Christopher

115879

Contents

About the Authors

Albert J. Geritz received his doctorate from the University of Missouri–Columbia. His essays on More, Rastell, and Daniel have appeared in *Moreana, English Literary Renaissance*, and elsewhere. An assistant professor of English at Fort Hays State University, he organizes the special sessions on "Thomas More and his Circle" each year at the International Congress on Medieval Studies, Western Michigan University.

Amos Lee Laine received his B.A. from Randolph-Macon College and his M.A. and Ph.D. from Duke University. He is now an associate professor of history at Hampden-Sydney College where he specializes in the Renaissance and Reformation. Professor Laine has presented numerous papers on the early Tudor humanists.

Editor's Note

The brother-in-law of Thomas More, the father-in-law of John Heywood, the great-grandfather of John Donne, John Rastell was a truly Renaissance man. As religious controversialist, government lawyer, legal defendant, entrepreneur, historian, antiquarian, patriot, playwright, printer, and theater designer, he brought to all his varied enterprises the boundless energy, bold experimentation, and pervasive morality that characterize the More Circle under the first Tudor monarchs. Rastell was, with Wynken de Worde and William Caxton, one of the most important English printers at the dawn of the Renaissance, while his device (more than theirs) with its juxtaposition of Christian and pagan images shows the sweep of his activity, the breadth of his imagination. Yet through a great range of endeavors, Rastell relentlessly wrote, compiled, translated, and published so as to teach—a humanist among humanists. In this first book-length study of the man and his literary works, Albert J. Geritz and Amos Lee Laine, a literary scholar and a Tudor historian, together fill in new facts and interpretations of this important beginning of the Renaissance. Their comprehensive review shows us how Rastell, withdrawing from More, was both Reformer and reactionary yet nevertheless, like More, served his government with loyalty, discipline, and fervor only to die ignominiously as a prisoner of state in the Tower of London.

Arthur F. Kinney

Preface

This critical survey of John Rastell intends to provide him the attention he deserves. It seeks to recount, revise, and add new insights to what is known about this middle-class citizen of sixteenth-century England and his efforts to apply humanistic concepts to the lives of "average" Englishmen in order to improve the commonwealth. Its purposes are to expand the knowledge and appreciation of his interlude(s), give his prose works on history, religion, and law close analysis, and ascertain his position as a humanist.

The achievements of his brother-in-law, Thomas More, and other illustrious members of More's Circle have too long overshadowed Rastell's accomplishments. Although such comparisons bring some attention to Rastell, they often make it all too easy to overlook the worth of this man who was more than the father of the first editor of More's English works, the father-in-law of John Heywood, and the great-grandfather of John Donne. Filled with the diverse interests so much a part of the Renaissance, Rastell's interlude(s), history, involvement in religious controversy, publication of books, legal treatises, attempts to sail to the New World, and many other projects merit careful examination.

Although such examination has not been totally neglected, twentieth-century criticism of Rastell is scattered throughout chapters of books, journals, and unpublished dissertations, and is not easily accessible. Yet mention of him in standard literary histories, the inclusion of his works in anthologies, and many journal articles reflect his secure status as a minor figure. The greatest stimulus to Rastell studies began in 1926 with Reed's *Early Tudor Drama*; while *The Four Elementis*, his printing ventures, and intriguing life have repeatedly provided the focus of much scholarship. His prose works and stance as a humanist and literary critic have been examined less frequently, an oversight this study hopes to correct. A reliable comprehensive edition and clarification of his canon would further aid in reassessing his literary merit as well as counter the assumption that early Tudor literature is dull, unentertaining, and dogmatic. The recent quincentennial of More's birth simultaneously revived questions previous scholarship raised about Rastell and created new ones.

This study answers some of those questions and poses new ones—all in an effort to enhance Rastell's reputation.

One chapter focuses upon Rastell's dramatic productions. Attributed to him without question, his best-known drama, *The Four Elementis*, adapts morality play structure to fit the needs of the Tudor interlude. Its combination of serious matter about geography, cosmology, and exploration with comic episodes to teach a primarily secular rather than a theological lesson is discussed as a bold experiment, and a close reading stresses its importance as a transition between religious and secular drama. Although Rastell printed *Calisto and Melebea* and *Of Gentylnes and Nobylyte*, these interludes cannot be attributed to him without question. In spite of this uncertainty, many ascribe all or part of them to him, and they are included in this study. The question of *Calisto*'s genre is intriguing, so this play, the first in English about passionate, illicit love, is viewed as a translation-synopsis-adaptation of the Spanish *La Celestina*, a morality play with an exhortation to virtue, an interlude with sophisticated dramatic and rhetorical entertainment for a courtly audience, a romantic-realistic drama, and a prototype of tragicomedy. *Gentylnes*, a dialogue-debate among a Knyght, Marchaunt, and Plowman on the *topos* of true nobility, receives close attention, and the ambiguities of its characters and themes indicate the complexities of what, at first sight, appears to be a rather simple play.

Another chapter considers Rastell's major prose works, *The pastyme of people* and *A new boke of Purgatory*. An ambitious historical treatise, *The pastyme* covers events from Creation to 1485 and combines medieval notions of historiography with Renaissance humanism to teach secular lessons about good governance and man's duty to serve the state. Its woodcuts of English kings, European rulers, and popes employ symbols to aid in teaching these lessons and to cast humanistic, moral judgments upon each temporal and spiritual leader's achievement. This chapter also explores the influence of Rastell's legal training and reading of classical, medieval, and Renaissance histories as well as More's *Utopia* on this new field of endeavor. His last major work, *A new boke of Purgatory*, is seen as a significant part of the religious controversy of the English Reformation. Since the tract is cast as a dialogue-debate between a Christian and a Turk, it is examined in reference to the long tradition of dialogue-debates in classical medieval literature. Its ironies, produced in ways similar to *Utopia*, also receive notice. Finally, this chapter on Rastell's rarely studied prose works relates the ideas they contain to his age.

The first chapter outlines Rastell's life and times, emphasizing those events that influenced his thoughts and endeavors. The accent falls upon his association with More's Circle, his attempt to reach the newfound lands, his printing house, his legal career, his interests in drama, his involvement in the purgatory controversy, and his ever-present concern for the good of the commonwealth. The last chapter concentrates mainly upon his prefaces, especially those of his infrequently read legal treatises, which often define his position as a humanist, his concern for translating as a means of enabling the English language to express more complex concepts, and his desire to stimulate the growth of a native, vernacular literature by looking to the past achievements of English writers. In an attempt to determine his merit, this chapter concludes that his life and works must be admired for their potential greatness, restless energy, bold experimentation, and active interest in educating the citizenry of the English commonwealth. These qualities have earned him a place of esteem in the history of English letters. The book concludes with a selective bibliography containing an enumeration of modern editions and secondary materials of value in the study of Rastell.

We gratefully acknowledge grants from Fort Hays State University and Hampden-Sydney College. The Pepys, Bodleian, and British libraries offered inestimable opportunities to examine the original editions of Rastell's works and other helpful assistance. Our typists proved themselves patient. We are also indebted to numerous scholars whose comments, essays, and books can only receive a small portion of the acknowledgment they deserve in our notes and bibliography.

Fort Hays State University   Albert J. Geritz

Hampden-Sydney College   Amos Lee Laine

Chronology

	formation Parliament by the Cornish borough of Dunheved. Beginning of association with Cromwell.
1529–1530	In France for six months, seeking academic support for king's divorce.
1530	*A new boke of Purgatory.*
1533	Frith's answer to *A new boke of Purgatory* converts Rastell to Protestantism. Becomes a zealous Protestant. Bill of 1533 proposes him as first master of the newly secularized Christ Church or the Priory of Holy Trinity, Aldgate.
1534–1535	Religious zeal revealed in three letters of supplication to Cromwell about printing proposals; one anticipates the *Book of Common Prayer.*
1535	Attempts to convert the monks at Charterhouse in London. Imprisoned after arguing that clerics should not receive tithes.
1536	20 April, Rastell makes his will, in which he names Henry VIII as one of the executors. 25 June, probable date of death.

Chapter One
The Life of John Rastell

John Rastell grew up in Coventry, the ancestral home of the Rastells, but London may have been his birthplace. During the fifteenth century Coventry, a leading industrial, trading, and financial center, witnessed the development of a vigorous civic spirit which manifested itself in economic, political, religious, and cultural activities. Coventry also figured prominently in the War of the Roses, when both Yorkists and Lancastrians sought to dominate this prosperous, autonomous town located near the domain of the earl of Warwick, the kingmaker.[1] Of interest to political leaders of the time was the influence exerted by the guilds in the civic life of Coventry. These societies utilized their members' wealth and effort to promote commercial interest, maintain peace, establish schools, stage pageants, and support chaplains. Guilds like the Trinity and Corpus Christi had wide influence both within the city and its environs and in other sections of England. Rastell thus suffered no provincial upbringing. Like Shakespeare, he matured in a district which boasted a traditional interest in "things of the mind."[2] The yearly cycle of civic ceremonies, guild festivities and observances, pageants and plays, could hardly have failed to influence the impressionable Rastell.

The Coventry Years

Before the birth of John, two generations of Rastells had participated in the civic life of Coventry when it was at its height of prosperity. His grandfather, Thomas, served in various capacities: warden, member of the Mayor's Council, collector for the King, and committeeman.[3] The grandparents, both members of Trinity Guild,[4] in 1461 provided financial aid for the Yorkist army fighting against the Lancastrian forces. John's father, Thomas, in addition to various civic posts, had legal responsibilities and served on commissions to settle land disputes and helped alleviate the financial difficulties of Coventry resulting from the defeat and death of Warwick in 1471. From 1478 until 1481, the elder Rastell served with Sir Thomas Lyttelton on a commission for Warwickshire.[5]

There is no extant record of Rastell's birthdate, and the date is deduced from a 1489 entry in the Corpus Christi Guild Book when Joan Symonds, widow of an ex-mayor of Coventry, paid the first installment of his guild fee. As admission to a guild usually occurred when a youth reached fourteen, 1475 is the supposed year of Rastell's birth.[6] His early education remains obscure, but there is a reference to Oxford.[7] Another source calls Rastell, "*litteratus*," implying he was liberally educated in mathematics, philosophy, theology, history, geography, and all literature.[8] The choice of a profession undoubtedly resulted from the legal and political activities of his family. Following several years in London as a member of the Middle Temple,[9] he returned to Coventry to pursue a career patterned after those of his father and grandfather.

The prominence of the Rastell family in Coventry's civic life enabled the young lawyer to enter immediately into public service, and records show his participation in several Chancery suits and membership on commissions to settle land disputes.[10] These posts indicate his life's occupation early became intertwined with service to the state: there was family precedent for such service, and Rastell conformed to precedent when he succeeded his father as coroner of Coventry.[11] During his tenure as coroner, Rastell also presided over the Court of Statute Merchant and acted as clerk of recognizances of debts. In such capacities, he participated in chancery suits, managing to demonstrate interest in social reforms, especially those concerning public grazing rights and supervision of schools by the laity rather than the clergy. As an indication of his efforts to champion the plight of the lower classes, he sided with the common citizens against the established hierarchy of church and wealthy burghers in most cases.[12]

In 1507, a wealthy merchant, Richard Cooke, appointed Rastell an overseer of his will, in which he bequeathed "One Bible in English" to Trinity Church in Coventry and Walstall Parish Church. This Bible (thought to be the Wycliffe version)[13] was certain to attract notice in Coventry, where Lollards had been burned and citizens were divided on religious issues such as lay control of their children's education. That Cooke should have considered Rastall a man whose religious beliefs would insure execution of his will indicates that the young lawyer possessed radical, if not Lollard, views. Accordingly, the

older Rastell was to question traditional beliefs to the extent of break-
ing with the established church. His resignation from civic posts in
1508 and move to London might have resulted from his involvement
with this controversial will.[14]

On the whole, the Coventry years were good ones. Rastell's
marriage produced three children, John, William, and Joan. His
legal and political experience earned him a good reputation as a
lawyer. He made contacts with prominent people who would, later
in London, assist in the projects suggested by his imagination. Certainly, his wealth increased. But especially important to Rastell's
development were the political, intellectual, and cultural influences
of Coventry's active guilds; indeed, his later life reflects the same
concern for the common good which characterized these guilds.

The More Connection

Aside from life in Coventry, the most significant factor in shaping
Rastell's character and career came from association with Thomas
More, his family, and friends. Little is known of the relationship
between the two brothers-in-law. How they met, their reactions to
each other, the depth of their friendship, the interchange of ideas,
the conviviality of the two families, both of whom played important
roles in early Tudor England, must remain matters of conjecture.

The earliest record of any contact between the two is an entry in
Henry VIII's *Book of Payments* which states that in 1499 Rastell,
More, and his father, John, joined another person to furnish securities
to repay a debt of 100 marks.[15] Why Rastell would be financially
connected with the Mores remains a mystery, but they met their
obligation by the next year. Perhaps More and Rastell met and
became friends while law students. Rastell, the older by three years,
was at Middle Temple when More was as Lincoln's Inn. Doubtless
through this connection, Rastell met More's sister, Elizabeth, whom
he had married by the time of his return to Coventry.[16] Relations
between the families, in the beginning, seem cordial and on at least
one occasion More traveled to Coventry. This visit furnished the scene
for his delightful account of a dispute with a friar. While the event
may not have occurred as More told it, his passing reference to his
sister is of interest here.[17] Thus by marriage, Rastell had become a
member, however peripheral, of the More Circle.

The term "circle" includes those individuals who shared More's interest in humanism. The ideas of Erasmus, Colet, Vives, Linacre, and Grocyn served as inspiration for intellectual activity. Their influence prevailed far beyond the immediate circle of their acquaintances. Indeed, this group profoundly influenced the law, government, drama, and education of Tudor England.[18] Because their ideas were attractive—and, at the time, notorious—they, of course, influenced Rastell. How well Rastell knew people like Erasmus is unknown.[19] It is tempting to suppose that Rastell met Erasmus during the latter's visits with More; indeed Rastell could have known all of More's friends. To what extent he was accepted as an equal in their circle is unknown. However, as a consequence of his connection with this group, he did absorb many ideas. It is possible to see in his activities the working out in practical terms of some idealistic projects of the humanists around More.

This is not to say Rastell lacked originality; rather, he possessed a less brilliant mind and wisely followed the lead of superior intellects. Though often immoderate and less than successful in translating thought into action, he nevertheless sincerely espoused the ideas of the More group: their emphasis upon humanist education for men and women of all classes; their desire for a rejuvenation of Christianity; their praise of mind over body; their reverence for law and the English legal profession; their enthusiasm for man's ability to explore and know the world as created by God; and, above all, their belief in the duty of an educated man to pursue actively a life of service to his prince in order to serve the commonweal.

The connection with More may have also figured in Rastell's move to London, though its date and reasons are obscure. Certainly the economic ills besetting Coventry around the turn of the century encouraged Rastell to seek a more secure environment for his family.[20] Perhaps the move seemed attractive because of the increasing association with the More family, an association offering opportunities for the satisfaction of Rastell's ambitions. From a financial standpoint, Rastell could afford to make the move, as he had profited from the will of Joan Symonds.[21] Perhaps a complicated mixture of these and other motivations, the move was probably a gradual process completed by 1510.

The relocation brought changes in the career of Rastell, who until this time had practiced law and served in legal capacities. He doubtless had other interests, but he was settled in Coventry and these remained unrealized. Apparently the opportunity to work with a former Coventry associate, Sir Edward Belknap, influenced him to move. Belknap, privy councillor to both Henry VII and Henry VIII, held many governmental appointments. One such venture occurred during the French War of 1512–14 when Rastell performed various services. In December 1514, he served as overseer for unloading "at the Tower of eighteen hoyes lately comen from Calais with the Kinges ordenance and fare cartes."[22] In the same month, again at Belknap's appointment, he oversaw the unloading of armaments from Calais into the Tower.[23] The documents describe him as a gentleman under whom carpenters and laborers worked. Such enterprise may seem incongruous for a lawyer, but Rastell, an active citizen of an England which encouraged versatility, undertook many unusual tasks.

The Printer-Publisher

His emergence as a printer shortly after the move is indicative of this versatility. The origins of his interest in this avocation, soon to become a second vocation, remain obscure. Yet of the many activities undertaken by Rastell, that of printer best illustrates the influence of More and Christian humanism distilled by his own concepts of service to the commonwealth. As a lawyer and a peripheral member of More's Circle, he shared their belief in education as the answer for all the day's ills. If there was anything held in more contempt by More and his friends than the vulgar display of wealth and nobility, it was uncritical public opinion.[24] Most members of the Circle were engaged in professions that offered them the opportunity to indulge in philanthropic propaganda for the education of the general public. These men—who had access to a universal language (Latin) and printing presses—belonged to the first generation of humanists, whose ideas had influence through the printed word. In addition, they suffered no restrictions of a guild system but were free to invest in the printing trade. For the early English printers, therefore, their work usually represented "a combination of a learned profession and a capitalistic venture."[25] Using such a definition, Rastell ably epitomizes the middle-class professional man whose ideas of humanism with its contempt for the clerical and aristocratic monopolies previously held in education, diplomacy, the arts, and law[26] led him into printing as a profitable means of liberating the masses.

The printing trade came late to England. Twenty-one years after

Gutenberg completed his edition of the Bible in 1455, Caxton set up a press in Westminster. To enter into this vocation could prove precarious because no certain reading public was known by the end of the fifteenth century. The English market for books was, indeed, small at the beginning.[27] While literacy by 1500 was no longer confined to the clergy, the reading public was not yet numerous enough to encourage many to venture into this uncertain profession.[28] Some, however, did succumb to the lure of profit or the desire to be influential in the development of a service; but almost without exception they did so only as a secondary occupation. Young people rarely could manage the extra money needed to finance this new art; instead, foreigners and older, more established Englishmen became printers—men like Caxton, a dealer in manuscripts and imported printed books; Plantin with his leather goods, prints, maps; Pynson, a pouchmaker; Raynold, the physician; and the Rastells, father and son, who practiced law.

These early printers functioned both as publishers and salesmen and often translated or even wrote their own books. Yet they were not totally independent because they relied upon the Continental printers and founders for supplying type and paper.[29] Even so, sales could not always offset the cost involved. Any printer who dared for whatever altruistic, humanistic reason to enter the profession had to cover some of the cost with earnings from other fields. Few printers could hope to make a fortune; they had to go into printing for other, less selfish, reasons.

Rastell's motivations demonstrate his humanistic orientation. He printed legal treatises, religious and controversial tracts, jest books, and popular plays, with little regard to whether the public tastes corresponded to his own. His aims had to be connected with the More Circle's ideas of education or at least the concept that the humanist was responsible for presenting the public with the material which would somehow seduce them onto the rational paths of humanism. In one of his prefaces, Rastell says that "the unyversall people of this realm had greate plesure and gave themself greatly to the redying of the vulgare Englyssh tonge."[30] Perhaps he sincerely believed this to be the truth (though recent studies disprove this assertion),[31] but most of his confidence must be credited to publisher's propaganda.

The exact locations and numbers of Rastell's presses remain uncertain. Probably his earliest printed work was More's translation of

The lyfe of Johan Picus erle of Myrandula (*STC* 19898a).[32] The title page bears the title, author, and "emprinted by Johan Rastell," but no date, though 1510 seems likely. However, the last page states, "Emprynted at London by Johan Rastell dwellyng at ye flete bryde at the aboot of Wynchecombe his place" (G4ᵛ). Someone else may have done the printing for Rastell, since there are no records of any other works published from this address. Sometime between 1510 and 1519 Rastell had clearly established a printing house at the "south syde of paulys"[33] where he published the bulk of his legal tracts. The earnestness with which he produced the *Liber assisarum* [Book of Assizes] (*STC* 9599), Fitzherbert's *La Graunde Abbregement* (*STC* 10954) with his introduction, *Tabula prime partis* [Table of Primary Parts] (*STC* 10955), and *An Abridgment of Statutes* (*STC* 9518) suggests his earlier foray into this profession had succeeded in convincing him of its lucrative benefits. More contemplation of the value of legal printing as a humanistic service to the commonwealth doubtless bore on Rastell's decision to become a professional printer.

Two types of printing houses surrounded St. Paul's: a "booth" or shop for both the printing and sale of books, and a combined dwelling and shop.[34] Rastell chose the latter kind when he moved from "South syde of paulys" to "Chepeside at the syne of the Mere Mayde next to Paulys Gate" in 1520. At the "south side of paulys" he must have had a boothshop, but the new quarters were more elaborate, because he began leasing parts of his dwelling shop to booksellers or printers as early as 1520.[35] Rastell's restlessness seems to have precluded any prolonged periods of printing. Apparently he cared little about the technical operations of the printing house; indeed, he seems seldom to have been more than an editor and publisher,[36] and was content to leave all practical work to his assistants. For months he lived at his country house at Finsbury Fields while subletting part of his dwelling-shop.[37] At first the house remained shut up during these absences, but by 1523 he began to sublet certain areas, retaining others for his use. Most of the tenants, in fact, were at one time his apprentices, a fact attesting to Rastell's good relations with his workers. Further evidence of this is the bequest in his will leaving his printing house to his workers.[38]

A problem in determining the extent of Rastell's role in printing revolves around his colophons. In some works, like *Of Gentlynes and Nobylyty* (*STC* 20723), "Johēs rastell me fieri fecit" may imply authorship; but for *Calisto and Melebea* (*STC* 20721), he uses the words "Johēs rastell me imprimi fecit." Reed has suggested that the latter colophon best translates as "John Rastell (the compyler) had me put in print."[39] This argument arose from a study of the colophon for Rastell's edition of Sir Thomas Linacre's grammar book[40] in which Henry VIII grants the "compyler thereof" the privilege of printing the work for eleven years. Clearly here Rastell himself wrote, compiled, translated; in other cases, however, he merely published, often with printing assistance from Gough or others, the work of other authors or translators.

The Mermaid printing house derived its name from Rastell's printer's device. This device seems to have been unique,[41] but other printers who subleased printed under it because a good sign was a valuable asset.[42] Actually, Rastell employed two devices. One featuring his monogram upon a ribbon with the motto "Justicia Regat" ("Justice Reigns")—and dating from the *Liber Assisarum* of 1513— obviously seemed attractive to him because it emphasized his legal and humanistic motivations. A larger, more detailed, device appeared with his move to the Mermaid. Depicting the four elements of earth, water, air, fire, the device draws heavily on Rastell's scientific interests, particularly astronomy.[43] The scene depicts the Almighty Father above the word *fiat* blessing his creations below: the stars and planets, moon and sun; the curved earth showing hills, buildings, trees, water, clouds, fire; and amid these elements, a merman and mermaid. The two half-human figures arise from the water and support a rectangular tilting shield with his monogram. At the bottom appears a scroll bearing his full name. In the corners on either side of the Almighty are shields bearing the Royal Arms of England and the badge of the Prince of Wales. Its inclusion poses a problem because no such person existed during the time of Rastell's printing. Perhaps assuming in 1520 that Queen Katherine would bear the king a son, the printer sought to win royal favor. Regardless, the device presents a collage of Rastellian beliefs and influences— a juxtaposition of Christian and pagan images, the concept of four elements, the love of astronomy, and the penchant for courting good fortune by flattering the crown.

Rastell delegated the mechanics of printing to assistants and apprentices, and only concerned himself directly with editing and publishing. There is, however, one notable exception. He may have taken an active part in printing Fitzherbert's *La Graunde Abbrege-*

ment, called "one of the finest examples of the sixteenth century printing."[44] The effort involved in the publication of the three folio volumes must have required considerable work. Its small secretary type, used by Rouen printers for service books, raises questions about foreign influence. Because secretary type admirably accommodated the close printing necessary for Law French, he may have chosen it, though he may have elected to have this important book produced abroad.[45] Such a charge, however, cannot be proved; indeed, the founts, brought from France and used by Rastell in 1513, were still in his possession as late as 1528.[46] The connection with the Rouen printers may further indicate that he learned his trade at the Norman presses.[47]

From a technical standpoint, Rastell's press rates an honored place in the history of printing music. Early printers discovered music to be a challenge because of the problems involved in getting notes on staves and words between staves without at least two printings.[48] The use of two or three impressions for music created beautiful books, but books which were, of necessity, limited to small editions because of the high cost of production. Only by inventing a method using one impression could the economic difficulties be surmounted. This new typographic principle cast each note as a separate unit with the adjacent portions of the stave attached to the note. When and by whom this was done is unknown, but sometime before 1530 several examples[49] of one impression printing appeared from English presses.

Probably Rastell may be given credit for using this revolutionary single impression method. Two pieces of music exist which bear his colophon. Though neither bears a date, they are assigned to the late 1520s, thus making Rastell one of the earliest English printers of music produced in one impression.[50] One of the pieces is a fragment copy of a ballad for one voice, the author or composer of which is unknown. There is no evidence that Rastell wrote either words or music; yet, with his surprising talents, he may have done both.[51] The music is as undistinguished as the four-stanza ballad telling of the tragedy endured by a young man whose lady has forsaken him. Bearing the punning title "Away mornygne" (*STC* 20700.3), the ballad ends on an optimistic note:

> . . . For all my cost yet for all
> that I trowe

> I have perchaunce. A fayre ryddaunce. And am
> quyt of a shrew.

The other music, more closely tying Rastell to printing, occurs in his *A new interlude and a mery of the nature of the iiij elements* (*STC* 20722). This is a song of six lines with the refrain, "Tyme to pas with goodly sport."[52] Printed on three pages, the one-voice music and words are followed on a fourth page by three lines of music for instrument alone or as voice accompaniment. Since this interlude contains so many of Rastell's ideas about humanism, capitalism, and patriotism, he probably considered it especially important and closely supervised its printing. If he did, then his involvement in developing a revolutionary method of printing music demonstrates the importance of his contribution to the history of printing as a whole. Even if he did not have direct contact with the printing, both pieces of music were produced from his press, where he was accustomed to subletting to men whose later printing careers proved important.[53]

Because others utilized Rastell's press and appropriated his printing sign to procure public approval, there have been problems in determining what he printed. For example, John Stanbridge's *Accidentia* bears no date but does state in the colophon, "Imprynted in chepe syde at the syne of the meare mayde."[54] Because of Rastell's interest in education and his connection with the More Circle, scholars have credited him with publications like *Accidentia*, a grammar book on the parts of speech in Latin. Similarly, four pages from *The boke of the new cardys*, a method of using playing cards to learn English and numbers and arabic figures, has been assigned to his press, not only because of his interest in such educative methods, but also because its type is used in his *Liber assisarum* in which he urges readers "To rede trewly the numbers of algorisme."[55] Or again, because he published *A. C. Mery Tales* (*STC* 23664) and *The Widow Edyth*, Rastell has been credited with *The boke of a hundred riddles* (*STC* 3319),[56] whose type does seem similar to other Mermaid works even though only a fragment exists today. Similarly related to the jestbooks are two sheets containing a poem in octave stanza, entitled *Fabyle's Ghoste*, seemingly printed by Rastell in 1533.[57] Another work often connected with his press, *Of Saint Margaret the blissed lef that is so swete*,[58] does not fit any category Rastell published. This does not preclude his publication of it, but his known printing, done for a public only then becoming aware of the ideals of the humanists, does not include such an orthodox medieval religious work. If he did publish it, such an exception is characteristically unpredictable.

Of equal curiosity to Rastell's bibliographers is the recently dis-covered remnant of a metrical version of the life of Becket bearing Rastell's device and stating that it was printed "in chepe syde next to Paules gate."[59] From the eight pages extant, a case may be made for his attempt to follow in his brother-in-law's footsteps and produce a secular history. Although his involvement with this publication remains unknown, the fact that it appeared from his press further demonstrates the influence of More and the humanistic ideal.

From an educative standpoint, Rastell's edition of Chaucer's *The parlyment of fowles* (*STC* 5093)[60] proves interesting, particularly because of a five-verse introduction attributed to its printer. Perhaps he planned to produce a complete edition of Chaucer. If so, it is unclear why he picked *The parlyment of fowles* first and never fin-ished the project.

William Harrington's *Comendacions of matrymony* (*STC* 12801) raises other questions. A copy exists without title page and date, yet it ends with the statement, "per Johane Rastell." Did Rastell actually print this? Did an apprentice print it with Rastell's knowledge? Without it? Why a book about a cleric advising matrimony? Is it humanistic? Because Polydore Vergil authorized the first edition, did Rastell have some scheme in printing another edition? The work clearly is from the Mermaid press, but all else is conjectural.

Such is not the case with John Thibault's *Pronostycacyon of the yere M.CCCCC.XXXIII* (*STC* 23952).[61] Although only a fragment exists, without colophon asserting printer's name, abode, or device, its type of print and content lend credence to the view that Rastell produced this book of almanacs and astrological predictions. Like his contemporaries, he felt no contradiction between a belief in divine causation and an attachment to the influence of the heavenly bodies. With his interest in scientific experimentation and exploration, he had a respect for the stars. Thus, he could enthusiastically publish Thibault's work.

Another undisputed publication from Rastell's press was *De octo partibus orationis* (*STC* 7012) by Aelius Donatus, grammarian and rhetoric teacher of classical times. Little is known about this publi-cation except for the Latin statement that it was printed by Rastell.

Perhaps he was interested in Donatus because of the English humanists' emphasis on Latin grammar as the basis for a liberal education.
Easily recognized as a product of More's influence and Rastell's own
ideas of public service was the publication of Thomas Linacre's grammar book. One of the most influential of the humanists, Linacre was
not merely a man of letters but a medical doctor with entree to the
royal person. This practical man accepted Colet's invitation to write
a Latin grammar for the boys at St. Paul's School, a notable center
of humanistic education. The grammar proved too scholarly for students, and Linacre felt offended at the outcome of his labor.[62]
Perhaps More persuaded his brother-in-law to print the grammar, for
which More wrote a prefatory poem. The book is printed in clear
type and on stiffer paper than usual,[63] suggesting that Rastell—
whether out of regard to the commonweal's good or with a view to
increasing profits—took special care with this work.

Further evidence of More's influence can be seen in the jestbooks
published by Rastell. Again, Rastell's motivations may have been
two-pronged, for not only were jestbooks popular with a public more
eager to be entertained than to read scholarly tomes, but wit and
satire already had proved indispensable to the humanists. The humanists advocated use of medieval exempla, illustrative tales employed
to elucidate points of doctrine.[64] Such aids proved invaluable tools
to men like Erasmus and More, who were working toward the
enlightenment of the reading public. The exempla, which in the
humanists' hands became jestbooks or merry tales, offered a proving
ground for nascent English prose fiction.[65]

More's household, noted as much for its happy spirit as for piety
and scholarship, spawned one such humorous book published by
Rastell: Walter Smyth's *The Widow Edyth: Twelve mery gestys
of one called Edyth, the lyeing wydow whyche still lyveth.*[66] Smyth,
a servant in More's household, wrote a humorous record of a widow
who uses her wiles to procure wealth at the expense of men of
noble and low stations.

Rastell himself was probably responsible for the other humorous
publication from his press, which became the "talk of the town"[67]
because of its prose anecdotes, some highly diverting, others grossly
obscene, and many aimed at the clergy. *A. C. Mery Talys*,[68] printed
a year after *Wydow Edyth*, shows a humanist bias with an English
patriotic twist. The compiler, possibly Rastell, gathered one hundred
stories from English folklore, apparently with little influence from

editions of current Latin and French tales.[69] Perhaps in one of his more patriotic moods Rastell determined to set into print some familiar tales, but to modify them to include new ideas of humor by ridiculing hypocrisy or ignorant acceptance of church belief. The tales educate through humor, point out simple lessons in gentility, and, above all, praise the individual's common sense, a gift to be prized over medieval logic-chopping. In contributing his bit to the molding of the new citizen, Rastell obviously did not envision an individual lacking in humor or warmth.

If Rastell's first printing was for More, one of his last also involved him. In 1529 More became embroiled in a controversy with Tyndale and the rising tide of Lutheranism in England. In response, More produced a *Dialogue concernyng heresyes* which Rastell published in June 1529.[70] More was particularly exacting in his demands and apparently disliked Rastell's handling of it, because in the fall William Rastell was commissioned to publish the *Supplicacion of soules*.[71] The elder Rastell, who by the 1530s was involved in legal work for the government and spending less time in the printing house, doubtless cared about serving his brother-in-law but had not taken the pains that More realized were needed in producing any literature dealing with heresy in those troubled days.

The Entrepreneur

Part of the capital necessary for Rastell's printing came to him through his association with Sir Edward Belknap. Knighted after the French campaigns, Belknap secured for his friend in October 1515 the lands, tenants, and debts of Richard Hunne, a well-publicized London heretic.[72] This wealth, however, carried the taint of anti-clericalism and the scandal surrounding Hunne's apparent suicide, rumored to be murder. Ironically, Rastell, in 1536, was to fall victim to the same controversy over tithes against which Hunne had rebelled with fatal results. But in 1515 he eagerly accepted as reward for his services Hunne's estate and the wardship of his two daughters whom Rastell hoped to marry to his sons in order to keep the dowries.[73] The marriages never took place, and Rastell never freely enjoyed his wealth. Because of the controversy connected with Hunne's death, complex lawsuits resulted from the grant. But however uneasily he held his claim to the wealth, he tenaciously fought to keep it because he had projects demanding heavy finances.

Most of Rastell's projects ended in lawsuits; he seems to have enjoyed legal controversy. His homes offer examples of his tendency to become involved in litigation. In 1515, he acquired two houses before he benefited from the Hunne indenture. At Monken Hadley, close to John More's manor at North Mymmes, Rastell leased a country house for thirty years; he also leased the nearby manor of Lydgraves for ten years.[74] Their proximity suggests a congenial relationship between the families. But regardless of his reasons for securing the leases, they embroiled him in lawsuits in 1519 and 1532.[75] Evidence from these suits reveals that he improved the land, refurbished the homes, devised baywindows and chimneys, and designed landscapes of well-stocked ponds and fair meadows between well-kept gardens. All these projects required money which the indenture of Hunne provided. Thus, Rastell lived as if to the manor born, even if he frequently lost the manor.

Perhaps the most costly scheme undertaken by Rastell resulted from the proximity of his home to More's. By no coincidence one year after More's publication of *Utopia*, his brother-in-law undertook an expedition not to the islands described by Hythloday, but to the New World. Financed by Hunne's wealth and securities from the royal treasury, the expedition set sail from Greenwich under royal letters of recommendation issued 5 March 1517 to Rastell and two other Londoners.[76] Credit for being the first Englishman to colonize the New World, however, eluded Rastell, who encountered mutiny shortly after leaving England. The successful lawsuit,[77] which he brought against his master mariner in November 1519, recounts the struggle between him and the crew who wished to use the provisions and the ship for pirateering. Off the coast of Ireland for some reasons, whether through the crew's cowardice or Rastell's refusal to cater to demands for certain provisions, the purser and master of the ship refused to go farther. While ashore at Waterford seeking new officers, he found himself stranded when his crew sailed to Bordeaux to sell the cargo. Thus ended one of the more significant projects of this Englishman who had envisioned colonization to the extent of carrying on board a London printer to establish printing in the New World.[78]

Rastell apparently had expected to be absent from England for about three years, because in 1534 he brought legal action against his brother-in-law, John Staverton, and Dame Alice, widow of John More, for mismanagement of his property during his absence.[79] In

1517 relations had been cordial enough when Rastell asked his in-laws to protect his family and estates; but, when his voyage ended in chaos and he did not immediately return, his in-laws evidently took a larger role in his affairs than he had intended. His interlude, *The Four Elementis*, which concerns geography and exploration, was a likely product of this period of isolation.

By 1520 Rastell had lost interest in printing, and had transferred his enthusiasm to designing and decorating dramatic presentations and public spectacles. How this ability originated and when he began to employ it is unclear. Perhaps Rastell observed and participated in the dramatic activities of the guilds in his youth in Coventry. The first evidence of this expertise comes from the flurry of correspondence in the spring of 1520 surrounding the preparations being made for the Field of the Cloth of Gold. This diplomatic extravaganza brought together many artisans and government officials whose duty it was to create buildings of sufficient grandeur for Henry VIII to impress Francis I. Belknap and Sir Nicholas Vaux, in charge of erecting the Great Hall at Guisnes, employed an army of artists, craftsmen, and laborers to execute the plans.[80] One of those employed was Rastell. In this assignment, Rastell revealed another surprising competence by helping to construct and paint the roofs of the banqueting hall, "curiously garnished under with knots and batons gilt and other devices."[81]

Rastell's work with the festivities at the Field of the Cloth of Gold must have been acceptable because he received a more important commission in 1522. In connection with the preparations being made for the state visit of the Holy Roman Emperor Charles V, the Court of Aldermen authorized Rastell to devise a pageant for the entertainment of the emperor as he and the king rode in the procession.[82] More himself participated in the procession, greeting the rulers, as Hall recounts, with "an eloquent oration" in Latin.[83] Perhaps this More connection was as influential for Rastell's commission as his garnishing of roofs at the Field of the Cloth of Gold.

Impressed by the commission, Rastell designed a pageant to be performed near his printing house. His plans were notable for mechanical gadgets to move scenery, suspend actors, and create special effects. The scene depicted "heaven curiously painted with cloudes, erges, starres of the Ierachies of angels."[84]

The extent of Rastell's involvement is uncertain. The cosmological setting and portrayal of the Father of Heaven surveying the singing angels suggest Rastell's printer's device. But responsibility for the set, props, actors' speeches, and direction of the pageant may have been delegated.[85] Perhaps Rastell only functioned as impresario, even though he had engineering experience. Regardless, the pageant seemed greatly to please the royal personages.

In spite of or because of such costly commissions, Rastell encountered financial difficulties by 1523. His voyage of 1517 had left him heavily in debt; by 1521 he owed 250 marks to the crown. At Michaelmas 1522, he also owed 810 marks in connection with the Hunne indentures. By failing to meet these obligations, he made himself vulnerable to his enemies. Through Belknap, Rastell had profited considerably. No doubt such reward aroused jealousy among those less favored. Probably the controversy over the Hunne affair would have subjected any new owner of the property to intrigue.

Using the Hunne estate as collateral, Rastell incurred debts he could not or did not meet. To liberate himself from one debt, he consented to the marriage of Margaret Hunne, one of his wards, to Roger Whaplode, the son of one creditor. The Whaplodes, upon realizing the extent of the Hunne estate, desired all, and on 4 May 1523 they obtained letters patent to "all Hunne's lands and tenements, and all leases and deeds relating thereto."[86] Perhaps Rastell's failure to repay the 1521 debt and the government's attempt to placate those displeased by the clergy's handling of the Hunne case may explain the crown's ruling. In any case, the Whaplodes presented Rastell as an opportunist who utilized the misfortunes of the martyr, Hunne. Further disadvantage to Rastell was the fact that Belknap, the real instigator of the 1515 grant, had died and could not defend his protégé.

Though in possession of letters patent, the Whaplodes failed to gain control of the estate, for Rastell fought them in several court suits. That one of the judges who reviewed the case in 1526 was Fitzherbert may help explain why Rastell, although fined several hundred marks in favor of the Whaplodes, retained the major portion of the Hunne estate.[87] Even in 1529 the problem had not been resolved; Rastell, however, eventually emerged the victor, probably because of his improved relations with Wolsey and family connections with More, made chancellor in 1529.

Undeterred by setbacks during his legal problems over the Hunne grant, Rastell proceeded with other interests. Certainly his quarrels with the government did not blight his career as a lawyer-administrator. In August 1523, he served as a "trenchmaker" under Charles Brandon, duke of Suffolk and brother-in-law to the king, and was also appointed a member of a commission to collect subsidy in Gloucester.[88] Knowledge of these activities makes Rastell's financial situation all the more confusing. He was not without income or means of employment, nor did he abandon pursuits entailing expense. And yet he refused or failed to meet some financial obligations. That he still possessed or hoped to possess wealth is evident from the fact that in 1524 he leased for forty-one years "1 acre 3 roods lying in the Lordship of Manor of Finsbury."[89] This area northeast of London was where wealthy persons built summer houses. That Rastell could move into this area and lease from the prioress of Holywell land which he drained by sewers and ditches indicates solvency and position.

It was at his Finsbury house that Rastell constructed "the earliest stage known to the historian of the Tudor drama."[90] Much information about this stage and dramatic activities at Finsbury comes from a lawsuit[91] of 1529–30. Henry Walton built the stage and was associated with Rastell in other theatrical enterprises such as the 1527 Greenwich pageant. In 1529–30, Rastell spent six months in France on government business, possibly seeking support for the divorce of Henry VIII.[92] During this time, Walton borrowed costumes and other properties assembled by Rastell and his wife for their Finsbury stage. Upon returning from abroad, the lawyer prosecuted Walton for damaged costumes and lost properties, whereupon Walton counterclaimed that Rastell had never paid for the construction of the stage. The lawsuit sheds interesting light on things theatrical in the early Tudor period.

The law records describe Rastell's stage as "board, timber, lath, nail, sprig and daubing,"[93] valued at 50 shillings. Probably no more than a covered platform, it served only as a place for actors to stand and be seen and heard. The illusion of spectacle emanated from the costumes. For these, Rastell paid dearly. The costumes were of green, blue, red, and yellow sarcenet decorated with colored embroidery and lined with red or blue buckram; some had capes of white cat fur. There were short garments of satin and chequered material, and various curtains, hangings, and draperies. Walton said the value of these was thirty-five shillings, nine pence; Rastell argued for about twenty shillings more.[94]

Because Rastell had an eye for profit, he lent these costumes for other performances, determining the rental according to whether the performance was a "stage-play in summer" or "interlude in the winter." The distinction seems to be that the stage plays were out of doors and prey to weather.[95] Obviously he used the drama not only for edification of his audience and the personal pleasure he derived from it, but also for income. His wife even helped to sew some of the costumes.[96] Therefore, these activities, while illustrating Rastell's inquisitive nature, nevertheless reveal a practicality necessitated by economic needs.

Rastell's interest in drama extended beyond his ventures as stage-owner and entrepreneur. Never hesitant to try his talents in a new field, he became a playwright-publisher. By the mid-1520s, his dramatic interest clearly influenced what he published. Prior publications had been legal in nature, but between 1525 and 1529 he published two plays he is thought to have authored: *Gentylnes* and *Calisto and Melebea.* These interludes may have been produced on his stage and seem to be products of his desire to illustrate significant problems. Obviously his litigious troubles did not preclude his occupation with such interests as drama.

Whether Rastell needed, for economic reasons, to produce books popular with the public or merely allowed his publishing to reflect his changing interests, by 1525 the output of his printing press reveals this shift in emphasis. Not only did he publish these plays, but also an older, more blatantly didactic interlude, *The Four Elementis.* This interlude, which reflects both his flair for the dramatic and unconventional presentation of his beliefs and concern for the commonwealth, extols the importance of geography and exploration for the English. Throughout his publishing career, concern for the needs of the public was Rastell's predominant motive for producing legal, dramatic, and ethical works.

Another indication of Rastell's growth in status was his connection with the festive spectacles that were an integral part of Tudor court life. In 1527 he again emerged as a gifted impresario for the entertainment at Greenwich of French ambassadors who came to arrange the Dauphin's marriage to Princess Mary. Preparations were undertaken with the painter Hans Holbein, who was commissioned to paint a mural.[97] Before this mural was to be enacted Rastell's pageant. For this task he employed the skills of some of those with whom he had collaborated on the Field of Cloth of Gold; he also pressed into service the builder of his Finsbury stage and his son, William.[98]

Rastell's theme for this pageant reflected his interest in cosmology.

As in his 1522 pageant, he worked with scenic effects featuring clouds, planets, and signs of the zodiac. Entitled "Father in Heaven," the 1527 pageant dramatized themes illustrated in his printer's device and reflected a blend of cosmography, fantasy, and religiosity that was common in Rastell's day. Featured in the pageant were cleverly designed canvases hanging from the roof and depicting the earth and, in rotation around it, the signs of the zodiac, the four elements, and the seven planets. Hall reports that "it was a cunnyng thing and a pleasant sight to beholde."[99] He continues by describing the interlude which took place among "lions, dragons, and greyhounds holding candlesticks, as more plainly appeareth in the reckoning of John Rastell," who also is credited with "the writing of the dialogue and making in rhyme, both in English and Latin."[100]

The Politician

When Rastell began his involvement in government service is unknown. Under Wolsey's chancellorship, his signature appears on Chancery bills, which had to be examined by lawyers who then reported whether the bills were worthy for royal consideration.[101] Such recognition suggests that his projects had not deterred his progress in the legal profession, nor had his financial troubles brought disgrace. In October 1525, as a beneficiary in a dissolution of the priory of Tichford in Warwickshire, he received seven acres of meadowland.[102] In government circles, undoubtedly, Rastell enjoyed prominence gained not by his avocations, but by his legal and administrative ability.

Again, Rastell's versatility is more remarkable when one considers that while executing plans for pageants, he was functioning as a publisher, government lawyer, legal defendant, writer, and devoted family man. His son, William, joined his father's activities during the Greenwich preparations and seems thereafter to have followed in his footsteps, taking law and printing as occupations. Between 1526 and 1530, the two Rastells published more legal studies, several plays, grammar books, and in 1529 Rastell's *The pastyme of people* (*STC* 20724). This survey of English history marks yet another facet of a remarkable career. After William moved to set up his own printing press in 1530, the father published little of note except his *A new boke of purgatory* (*STC* 20720), which precipitated the religious controversy leading to his death.

During the last years of Wolsey's chancellorship, Rastell's name is
mentioned frequently in government records as a member of a commission to determine the status of foreigners in the London business
world and as a supervisor for Gloucester.[103] Under More's chancellorship from 1529 to 1532, Rastell continued to take part in governmental legal service, in spite of the fact the relationship of the two
brothers-in-law had deteriorated by this time. Perhaps the death of
John More in 1530 weakened ties among his children, although
Rastell seems never to have been close to his in-laws.

More fundamental reasons for the break began in 1529 when
Rastell was elected to Parliament from the Cornish borough of
Dunheved.[104] This Reformation Parliament, so effectively manipulated
by Cromwell and the king, met until 1536 and brought about sep-
aration from the church in Rome. From the beginning of its sessions,
Rastell seems to have been more liberal in his religious-political
beliefs than More, who probably considered such liberal tendencies
signs of weakness. But if these facts lead one to class Rastell as an
English reformer, his actions in 1530 contradict this supposition.
Whether from family pressure or sincere conviction, he published
his defense of the doctrine of purgatory which he hoped would
assist More and John Fisher, bishop of Rochester, in their controversy
with Simon Fish, the author of *A Supplicacyon for the Beggars.*

Fish had attacked the purgatory doctrine, and More had defended
it with scriptural arguments. Fisher contributed a defense based on
patristic learning. Why Rastell felt obligated to add his defense is
uncertain. If he hoped to win More's approval or convert wayward
English Catholics, he failed in both quests. He sought to prove the
doctrine of purgatory from a position of reason without relying upon
scriptural or patristic authorities. The result was a dialogue resem-
bling the form of one of his published interludes but much less
entertaining. More and Fisher, it has been noted, "endeavored to
prove the fire, and Rastell the smoke, of purgatory."[105] Answering
this tripartite response to Fish, John Frith, a disciple of Tyndale,
attacked the positions of More, Fisher, and Rastell. Frith's attack was
so convincingly delivered that Rastell responded, although no copy
of this retort survives. Frith answered Rastell from the Tower, where
he was confined as a heretic. This 1533 answer, so brilliantly conceived, had the effect of converting the liberal Catholic lawyer to
Protestantism![106]

Rastell's shift from More's Catholic position to a Protestant one like Cromwell's occurred between 1530 and 1533, so the Frith debate may have only hastened this transition. It was during these years also that he broke with the More family and allied himself with Cromwell, so that Rastell was not hurt when More resigned, was arrested, and executed as an heretical traitor. Apparently Rastell was convinced that Cromwell, not More, was the social reformer destined to implement the ideas he had promulgated in his writings. Perhaps more than anything else, this judgment of human nature stands as his major flaw. As Reed aptly observed, "It was John Rastell, not More, who was the Utopian dreamer; but the masters he was serving were prosecuting not Rastell's schemes but their ends."[107]

Rastell proved himself a loyal servant to Cromwell, who gave him many duties. A bill of 1533 unsigned by Henry VIII proposes Rastell be made first master and governor of the newly secularized Christ Church or Priory of Holy Trinity, Aldgate.[108] The royal approval went instead to the new chancellor, Thomas Audley. Against such competition Rastell was a mere pawn. Cromwell, however, used him and another lawyer to investigate the "true making of deeds and indentures"[109] to check fraudulency in London. As sign of favor, in 1533 Cromwell included Rastell's name with his own on a list of ten men given a fifty-year lease on all lead mines in Dartmouth Forest.[110] A later entry, for December 1534, cites Rastell as one of the controllers of the lead monopoly who presented money to the king.[111]

Service with Cromwell on a royal commission to investigate taxes from Middlesex County[112] gave Rastell additional prominence in the early 1530s. And when in 1534 Cromwell appointed him to serve with Roland Lee, bishop of Lichfield and Coventry and his particular favorite, in quelling rebellion in Wales, [113] Rastell reached the zenith of his political career. This favor with Cromwell placed him in a position to exert influence. At least John Arundel thought so when in 1534 he wrote Rastell begging him "to move Cromwell to solicit the Bishop of Exeter"[114] to grant Arundel a section of land for lease.

As quickly as Cromwell could raise men to power, just as quickly could they fall. In spite of prominence and its remuneration, in 1534 Rastell suffered another of the financial crises which plagued him throughout his life. In this year he lost his home at Monken Hadley through a lawsuit over the 1515 lease. He brought suit against his brother-in-law, Staverton, and his mother-in-law for their manipulation of his property during his 1517 voyage and subsequent stay in

Ireland. Deteriorating family relationships or pressure from creditors to make good his debts may explain this long wait. Lee called him "a pore man" who was forced to sell all his Warwickshire property, thus severing his connection with Coventry.[115] Royal records for the next two years list him as owing some twenty pounds, in spite of the fees gained from his new administrative post.[116] In 1535, he and others, among them Richard Riche, owed payments to the king,[117] and in 1536 Rastell's name still appeared on a list of payments due to the crown.[118]

Rastell's Final Schemes

Following a pattern developed during his lifelong quest for additional income, in his last years Rastell fell back on his old avocation—printing. After 1530 his publishing business was dormant except for issuing reprints, particularly law books. Given the religious climate of 1534, it was Rastell's attempt to combine a return to printing with his career in government service that produced the tragedy of his last years, when, becoming embroiled in controversy over tithes, his obstinate, foolhardy actions led to imprisonment and death.

Early in 1534 he proposed a printing scheme to relieve his pecuniary troubles. But in addition to this motive, there was the purpose fundamental to all of his projects, service to the English commonwealth. In three extant letters to Cromwell, who had been appointed the king's secretary, Rastell reveals these schemes. The first letter relates to his role as a propagandist.[119] He had edited a book entitled *Boke of the Charge.* Previously he had given it to Cromwell for official approval before publication. Since it dealt with religious laws as they affected the courts, Rastell thought it prudent to have it sanctioned by his superiors before unleashing it on the public. Apparently Cromwell's delay in reviewing the matter disturbed Rastell, who pleaded to be allowed to explain its intent.

Rastell believed the book could be effective only if it had the approval of the king's commission and even Parliament. In a plea to Cromwell's sympathy for his appointees, Rastell asked Cromwell to recognize the book as the result of "great payn and study and labor" which had brought "nought but great losse and hyndraunce, to myself and hateyrd and dysdeyn." As if to remind Cromwell of the prominence his servant had attained as a loyal, anticlerical follower of royal policy, Rastell ended with the admonition that "if some which ye call priests and spyrtuall men though if they knew it come of me they for dysdeyn wolds do what they coulde to hynder it."

The second letter[120] reveals the secretary apparently had not heeded his petitioner's request. In this letter, Rastell again asked that his book be declared "among the people thoroh out all England." Having taken pains to prepare the book, Rastell requested permission to attend the council session or to be present if and when the king reviewed it to explain any difficulties. With much concern, Rastell pleaded for the life of his book not only to placate his creditors but also to fulfill a real service to ". . . the kyngs grace and the quietness of the people."

In a third letter[121] to Cromwell, Rastell lacked the self-confidence of the first two, in which he had presumptuously sought royal approval for a task well done. This letter contains the musings of an old man tired of being misunderstood and underrated. Cromwell had returned the *Boke of the Charge* with revisions which Rastell felt could be made in ten or twelve days with the collaboration of unspecified authorities. But before he grudgingly made the revisions, he wanted to impose two conditions: when the book was resubmitted for royal sanction, that he be permitted to be present to defend it, and if it was given "auctoryte of the kyngs comyssyon," that he be allowed to print and thus profit from it.[122] Because with the king's approval the book would be bought by all justices, the impoverished author had reason to expect hearty sales. A first printing of ten to twelve thousand[123] copies at 100 pounds would be sufficient for every shire to possess a few copies of it.

The remainder of this letter reflects a melancholy mood which may have been temporary and calculated for effect or may have resulted from his belief that he had suffered excessive setbacks. Rastell reminds Cromwell that for the past four or five years "I have spend my tyme and gyffyn my bysynes" for the "kyngs causis and oppressyng of the popes usurpyd auctoritie, and thereby gretly hyndered myn own bysynes."[124] Rastell's law practice declined from twenty nobles a term to forty shillings a year, his printing press from 200–300 reams of paper yearly to less than 100.[125] These reverses, Rastell reminds Cromwell, he had borne cheerfully because he had "longyd and leynyd unto your Maystership specyally before any other of the Kyngs Counsell." Rather pathetically, Rastell pleads for the recognition he felt his services and sacrifices merited.[126]

There follows what is probably a feigned position, although the last sentiment was undoubtedly sincere: "Syr, I am an Old Man. I loke not to lyff long, and I regard ryches as much as I do chypps, save only to have a lyffyng to lyff out of det; and I care as mych for worldly honor as I care for the fleyng of a fathyr in the wynd. But I desyre most so to spend my tyme to do somewhat for the commyn welth, as God be my Juge."[127] While Rastell was well aware of the role of flattery in Tudor government, he cannot be charged with total insincerity in this passage because his entire life attested to his efforts to put into practice these high ideals.

As the final suggestion, Rastell proposed a book of prayers in English "which be to bryng the people which rede them from the beleue of the popes neughty doctrine."[128] Such reforming zeal indicates how his religious change led him beyond the Protestant extremes to which Cromwell and his royal master cared to go. Never content with moderation, Rastell became a radical reformer. Among the bills Cromwell's lawyers chose for the king's consideration in 1534, some of Rastell's selections are significant. One of these bills proposes that English sermons written by government appointees be printed and distributed for weekly use in all parishes. In a bill of his own proposing, Rastell suggests printing official tracts to prove priests may marry, men ought not to revere images, and prayers for the dead have no value.[129] Such proposals, not in agreement with the king's beliefs, indicate the theological reversal of Rastell, who earlier defended all these beliefs.

Although he was disappointed by failure to publish his book, Rastell proceeded in his campaign of religious and political service. With Cromwell's knowledge, he took as his personal task the conversion of the monks in the London Charterhouse. In two letters to his master in spring 1535, John Whalley, Cromwell's agent, reported the activities of Rastell, who searched all the monks' cells seizing subversive books.[130] Such practice Whalley condemns as naive, believing few monks would be convinced to change their opinions. Rastell, however, attempted to preach to the monks.[131] And even though Rastell, according to Whalley, was well trained and meant well, he failed in his mission because the monks "laugh at all he says." This incident injured Rastell's already dubious fame as Cromwell's proselytizing agent.

Having incurred the ridicule of the clerical class, Rastell alienated Cromwell by opposing the government position on tithes and curates' fees. This controversy dated from the days of the Hunne case, when Rastell had profited from the death of this protestor of clerical tithes.

By the reformation Parliament, public opinion was decidedly against the high fees clerics collected from tithes. To win clerical support, Henry VIII submitted the question to arbitration by the clergy aided by Cromwell and others. In 1534 a compromise, not pleasing the now radical Rastell, settled the issue. Rastell stubbornly defied the royal proclamation concerning tithes, with the result that he was imprisoned.

Rastell was tried before Cranmer and his court. Arguing against tithes as a livelihood for clerics, Rastell insisted they should live off freewill offerings. The present compromise was unfair. As basis for his arguments he cited the laws of nature, man, and God expounded in his law books' prefaces. Upon questioning by the bishop of Winchester and Cranmer, Rastell persistently "sang again his old song."[132] Ironically, although he prided himself on his presentation of political philosophy, Rastell's arguments impressed none of his judges. When neither side gave ground, his obstinacy made Cranmer "weary."

Exactly how long Rastell was a prisoner in the Tower is uncertain, but for several months to a year he was confined as a dangerous person not under sentence of death. Sometime in late spring 1536, he wrote Cromwell a last letter.[133] From its tone, it is easy to believe the writer is a broken, probably sick, old man of sixty-one. In earlier letters to his former employer, although he had used the self-abasing tone of an inferior addressing a superior and resorted to flattery, generally he seemed hopeful that Cromwell, recognizing his value, would grant his petition. This confidence is not anywhere to be found in the 1536 letter. Rastell, who died within weeks after writing it, seems consumed by the despair of his pleadings for reprieve.

Without preliminaries, Rastell announced his letter was a plea for remembrance from a "pore prysoner." Protesting innocence of any crime against the king or laws of the realm, Rastell contended if allowed to plead his case he could win pardon. For too long he had been confined without due process of law. Even if the king or his council were not at leisure to hear the case, "at the lest me thynk the crume is not such but that I myght well have my pore carcase at lybertye." This kind of imprisonment was incomprehensible to the lawyer. He could not see how he could be of any profit to anyone by being bound in hard captivity where he could "do nothyng to get my proper lyvyng" but must rely on "almys and charyte." The last sentences, possibly the last words he wrote, reveal the depths to which this energetic man fell before his death. He again requested Cromwell to have "some remorse" and help him to obtain the equity of the king's law. His life rests in Cromwell's hands: "And if I be here at the Kyngs own commandment . . . that I can not be releasyd but by hys own most gracyous mouth, I may be here tyll I starve or that I can come to the Kyngs speech or fynde my frendys to speake for me unless that you extend your goodness toward me." In return, Rastell declared he would be Cromwell's bondsman "durying my pore lyfe" and signed this degrading letter, "By me now a myserable prisoner."

The end came quickly and, apparently, from natural causes. On 20 April 1536, Rastell made his will,[134] appointing the king and Ralph Cressey executors. Cressey reported the death on 25 June, but the exact date remains a mystery. Despite the circumstances under which it must have been composed, the will reflects ironic humor. Musing God's blessings have vanished with death, Rastell distributed his goods. To his wife he left his printing business, press, notes, and profits; to a friend and overseer of the will, Francis Bigot, twenty shillings; to his elder son William, forty shillings; to son John, five pounds; and to daughter Joan, five pounds. To his servants he bequeathed a table, a book, and small amounts of money. He strikes a wry tone as he leaves to "maister Crumwell for his good counsell to be had after my dethe to be paid as it may bee received of the sale of my bookis, v markes." The same kind of bequest went to the lord chancellor, Thomas Audley, "for spedy justice in my suits that shalbe befor hym." The will closes with an explanation for the choice of executors. Rastell chose the king and Ralph Cressey not as equals but because he felt the king, who had judged him guilty, needed someone to explain his crimes, and Cressey was that one. Henry renounced probate, and Cressey did likewise; thus on 12 October 1536, it was granted to Elizabeth, Rastell's widow.[135]

Elizabeth Rastell outlived her husband a year, during which she lived with her daughter, Joan, wife of playwright John Heywood and future grandmother of John Donne. William Rastell continued his careers as lawyer and printer of the works of his uncle More. The year of his father's death, the young John Rastell set sail and reached Labrador, thus achieving what had eluded his father.[136] The father Rastell, dubbed by some a "Lutheran,"[137] became a symbol of radical Protestantism. At a meeting of clerics at Doncaster in the year of his death, Rastell's name was included among those of others whose heretical writings should be destroyed—"Luther, Wyclif, Husse, . . . Tyndall, Barnys, . . . Raskell, Seynt Germayne, and such other heresies of Anabaptists."[138] Such a charge would have saddened Rastell who in all he had endeavored sought only to serve his fellow citizens of the English commonwealth.

Chapter Two
The Interlude(s)

The term interlude has never been clearly defined. Some understand it as a play enacted between the courses of a banquet or as an entertainment interpolated into a larger social context. Others look to etymology and argue that the entertainment, recreational activity, game, or "play" (*ludus*) was merely between (*inter*) two or more speakers. It is also possible the English spelling "enterlude" implies a false etymological association with entering: the players enter the hall and solicit the spectators' attentions. Recently some have asserted the medieval Latin title, *interludium*, attached to a fourteenth-century English comic wooing play, may be an attempt to dignify native traditions of secular "playing" with the banquet entertainments of classical Rome. Rastell himself contributes to the definition, although not from an etymological perspective. In a lawsuit around 1530 in which he was involved, a distinction between open-air "stage plays in the sommer and interludes in the winter" is made. Unfortunately, this distinction is not found elsewhere unless it is in a royal proclamation of 16 May 1559.

Whatever the reason for the adoption of the name, interludes are plays between two or more speakers. Taken as a part of English dramatic history, they are not merely "interludes" between *Mankind* and Marlowe, but plays with considerable theatric, thematic, and aesthetic value of their own. Brief in scope, they frequently turn on a single situation requiring about six players and little external action. Indoor performances generally occur in a single place occupied by actors together or in turns. Sometimes broken into two or three sections, they range from three-quarters to an hour-and-a-half long. Each is composed of elements taken from mystery, miracle, and morality plays; popular folk entertainments, such as tournaments, mummings, and civic pageants; classical and Continental traditions; Renaissance humanism; and other sources.

The Four Elementis

A New Interlude and a Mery, of The Nature Of The Four Ele-mentis,[1] a traditional morality play in structure and characterization, humanist and educative rather than religious in theme, intention, and auspices, is commonly attributed to Rastell. Probably written between 1517 and 1519, Rastell uses the morality form, interspersed with low-life comedy, song, and dance, to disguise and enhance lessons in cosmology, geography, and geology. Nature Naturata, Studyous Desyre, and Experyence attempt to teach Humanyte natural science by arguing that, through knowledge of "phylosophy naturall," man can know and love God more meaningfully. Sensuall Appetyte, Yngnor-aunce, and the Taverner, opposed to such education, try to distract Humanyte. In contrast to the traditional morality, in which good and evil struggle for man's soul, the intellect battles with the body in Rastell's work.

The only extant copy lacks several pages internally and at the end, and there is no colophon or other printing to indicate an author or date. Reed, however, presents substantial evidence for Rastell's authorship, noting John Bale, Rastell's contemporary, attributes it to him.[2] The play also refers to an abortive voyage to the New World, similar to Rastell's 1517 venture. In view of disappointed hopes and the consequent resentment, Rastell might well have begun writing it during his stay at Waterford where he had time to assemble the knowledge he had gathered from reading, studying maps, and talking to sailors and merchants.

Additional ideas, appearing in Rastell's other works, are not commonplace and argue for his authorship.[3] *The Four Elementis*, for example, concerns exploring the New World, exploiting its resources for the king's honor and the commonwealth's benefit, and converting its pagan inhabitants. Unlike some other humanists, Rastell had an ever-present interest not only in educating common men in the Bible, good conduct, and natural science, but also in developing the English language as the medium for achieving those goals. This emphasis on secular learning for the commonweal and as a spiritual tool is not found in the thought and writing of other More Circle members, and the *Elementis* stresses experience, reason, and common sense as opposed to formal teaching and study. No other drama of the More Circle employs a character like Experyence, who, simply because he has traveled in "many a straunge countree" (666) and

knows how to use "dyvers instrumentys" (392), has "grete fylycyte /
Straunge causes to seke and fynde" (667–68). In *The pastyme*,
Rastell discusses natural science and practical learning, like the cause
of the hot springs at Bath or the problems of weights, measures, and
money values. He also displays there and elsewhere his interest in the
commonweal. *A new boke of Purgatory* echoes an attitude characteristic of Rastell, for it stresses "natural reason and good philosophy"
as opposed to dogma and authority. The intellect is man's most noble
faculty, Rastell maintains, and accordingly, he presents the scientific
lessons of the *Elementis*. His major theme is to know oneself, one's
capacities, and thereby reach God.

Internal evidence establishes a date of composition. Experyence
points to a "figure," possibly a globe, and then refers to Cabot's voyages and his discovery of Newfoundland in 1499 (768–74).[4] Rastell
evidently regards Amerigo Vespucci[5] as the discoverer of the New
World and follows reputable contemporary geographers in claiming
1497 as the year of discovery. Thus, the reference to finding the New
World "within this twenty yere" (736) places the date of composition at about 1517.

To understand Rastell's intentions in *The Four Elementis*, one
must analyze the title page, in which he seemingly envisions performances for two sorts of audiences and cuts to suit the tastes of
each: "yf the hole matter be playde, [it] wyl conteyne the space of
an hour and a halfe; but yf ye lyst ye may leve out muche of the
sad mater . . . than it wyll not be paste thre quarters of an hour of
length." If these directives state the play's functions, themes, and intentions, their critical implications are significant. The playwright's
chief concern apparently is to instruct his audience in natural science[6]
and lure them, especially the lower-class segment, into the "school-
room" through dramatic entertainment. The play, therefore, intends
to teach and delight.

The author also writes simultaneously for high and low classes,
constructing his play for presentation where both would gather. By
designing it so much serious matter and some costly entertainments,
like dancing, can be omitted, he makes it suitable for touring and
low-class audiences. The full play, interlaced with humor and entertainment, was probably presented before the lower classes, perhaps at
Rastell's Finsbury Fields stage. Since a "dysgynge" may be given
"yf ye lyst," the full version required noble patronage. A disguising,
Bevington writes, "an outgrowth of Lydgate's courtly mummings and

predecessor of the Jonsonian mask, would obviously be intended for an indoor entertainment in which noble spectators . . . could dance."[7] Its call for dancing and minstrelsy resembles another early Tudor drama, Henry Medwall's *Fulgens and Lucres*,[8] which may have been performed under similar aristocratic auspices.

Furthermore, direct, informal references suggest Rastell has the same attitude toward his audience that Medwall exhibits in his dramas, and that he anticipates similar backing. The Taverner shoves his way through the spectators (555), who are asked to make way, just as those of *Fulgens* are asked to make room for the entrance of A (I, 193) and B (II, 75). Yngnoraunce makes a remark about the audience simultaneously confiding in and joking at them:

> For all they that be nowe in this hall,
> They be the most parte my servauntes all,
> And love pryncypally
> Disportis, as daunsynge, syngynge,
> Toys, tryfuls, laughynge, gestynge;
> For connynge they set not by.
>
> (1301–6)

This passage recalls Pryde and Sensualyte who, in *Nature*, brag to the audience and let them in on their plans, then jab at them by suggesting they know the way to the stews (I, 367–71). A and B in *Fulgens* occasionally confide in the audience (I, 910–11). Although the *Elementis* contains no further references to the audience, and although both *Nature* and *Fulgens* go to greater lengths to appeal to and involve their audiences, Rastell shares Medwall's attitude and cultivates a fairly close bond between the play and spectators. The circumstances of performance are similar for all three plays, and the action probably takes place in an area directly adjoining the spectators' seats. Certainly Rastell's use of the globe suggests that the spectators are close enough to see Experyence point to large land and water masses.

The shortened form of *The Four Elementis* deletes "muche of the sad mater": the Messengere's introduction, parts of Nature's introductory speech, and some of Experyence's lectures. Since no more specific directions are given, one may speculate upon what portions of "sad mater" might be omitted in the touring version, but one need not agree with the claim that Rastell may have dropped Experyence's

nationalistic plea for exploiting the New World's resources and converting its natives.[9] For an unlettered audience, Rastell possibly ex-
cluded other less appealing topics. Readily expendable are Experyence's repetitious proofs for the earth's roundness or fine points of
Nature's introduction to the elements. Apart from singing, no dancing or other entertainments were used in the touring version; thus,
enough of Experyence and Nature's speeches could be cut to reduce
the performance to three quarters of an hour and still provide the
unlearned audience with exciting information about natural science
and cosmology.[10] In fact, the shortened version focuses on Humanyte's
decision to study or not to study, and the low-life scences not only
delight low-class audiences, but also teach through plots similar to
those of the moralities. Cutting for popular audiences did not result
in farce, and the play's structure is unique, because it can be altered
to suit three audiences. The most stimulating of these combines the
lettered and unlettered, the upper and lower classes, and Rastell plays
the responses of such spectators to characters, situations, and themes
against each other.

     Unlike a "whole life of man" morality play,[11] no growth from
youth to age nor any grand conflict between the virtues and vices
occurs in *The Four Elementis.* Humanyte is presented allegorically as
the human intellect; Appetyte, on the one hand, and Desyre, Experyence, and Nature, on the other, struggle to win Humanyte's assent to a nonintellectual or intellectual way of life. The morality-
based drama traces Humanyte's progress from innocence to temptation and life-in-sin to repentance and final reconciliation.

     By understanding the importance of Humanyte's initiations into
learning, temptation, fall, and repentance, and by viewing the drama
as a lesson, complete with demonstrations interrupted with merry
scenes, Axton traces an alternating pattern of instruction about physics
(148–500) geography (659–878), and the earth's rotundity (1031–
1134) and "recesses" with Appetyte and his cronies. He believes its
"dramatic purpose is to clarify rather than present experience" and
that the "verbal instruction of Humanity is not inherently dramatic."[12]
From Medwall's *Nature,* a play he printed, Rastell might have copied
the morality structure, adapted it to a secular topic, and used it as a
method of alternating "sad" matter and merry conceits to provide
comic relief. Although some of the second repentance scene is miss-
ing, one can hypothesize that Humanyte here demonstrates his grasp
of the lessons imparted to him and declares that he now has the intel-

lectual equipment for a happy life. Humanyte and the audience have learned their lessons, and Rastell, the real teacher, realized that humor interspersed with instruction enhances instruction.

The play's prosody depends upon *Nature* in yet another way.[13] Initially, Rastell utilizes the twofold verse pattern consistently followed in *Nature*: the dignified, literary, heavy-lined rime royal stanza for serious portions, and a variety of light-lined, tail-rimed strophes for comic parts. However, after the initial serious portion, the rime royal does not appear again. The rest, serious and comic parts alike, includes less dignified stanza forms and even stanzas from popular songs and ballads. The play, however, contains several prosodic "firsts" of historical interest: the insertion of songs having their own verse patterns, a half-lined mock blessing, and a deliberately rimeless mock song of Robin Hood, "perhaps our earliest example of nonsense rhyme, a jumble of phrases from ballad and romance."[14] Rastell's mixture of serious and comic subjects and dignified and less dignified verse forms can also be seen in his use of language, chosen, on the one hand, from the Latinate and multisyllabic, and on the other, the plain and colloquial.

Character development in the casts of morality plays and morality-based interludes involves growth in separate classes: (1) neutral characters, (2) representatives of good, and (3) representatives of evil.[15] The *Elementis* has recognizable members of each class, but no truly evil characters; Yngnoraunce and Appetyte are only evil if they become excessive. Nature, Studyous, and Experyence are not especially interesting because of their dogmatic natures. As with other writers of moralities and morality-based interludes, Rastell faces the difficulty of making the "good" characters as dramatically attractive as the "bad" ones.

Humanyte, the neutral character, functions as a personified externalization of the problem every man confronts as he is torn between the forces of the body and the intellect. As a character, Humanyte, like the heroes of other moralities, is largely an allegorical, passive, often unmotivated, and easily manipulated, straw man. At the beginning of his first temptation (405–547), he maintains the reasoned spirit of inquiry he manifested, appropriately enough, during the lectures of Nature and Studyous. He interrogates Appetyte with calm open-mindedness, and his reaction to Appetyte's description of himself would win the approbation of every humanist:

> Than I cannot see the contrary
> But ye are for me full necessary
> And ryght convenyent.

(478–80)

Nor is there anything sinister or sinful in his decision to forego
Studyous's company:

> Syr, I pray you be contente.
> It is not utterly myne intente
> Your company to exyle,
> But onely to have communycacyon,
> And a pastyme of recreacyon
> With this man for a whyle.

(494–99)

Humanyte's submission to Appetyte comes only after the latter reveals his evil side:

> Ye shulde ever study pryncypall
> For to comfort your lyfe naturall
> With metis and drynkes dilycate,
> And other pastymes and pleasures amonge,
> Daunsynge, laughynge or pleasaunt songe;
> This is mete for your estate.

(510–15)

To a humanist, Appetyte, who is basically a neutral human power,
becomes sinful only when allowed to dominate. Appetyte offers Humanyte the prospect of uncontrolled sensual indulgence, and Humanyte gives him the control he requests (526–28). The first temptation,
then, is presented in strictly humanistic terms and involves the passive hero forgetting earlier lessons, depending solely on the impressions and whims of the moment, and deliberately, though thought-
lessly, choosing to give himself to bodily forces "for a whyle" (499).
Humanyte's second fall is similarly unmotivated, since no particular
excitement is generated in watching a student, whose only justifications
are ennui and bland relativism, fall into the clutches of sensuality
and ignorance. When Yngnoraunce asks why Humanyte bothered
with "losophy," he answers:

> ... when any man is
> In other mens company,
> He must nedes follow the app[et]yte
> Of such thyngys as they delyte.

(1211–14)

To the irrelevant question, where did you find better cheer, Humanyte responds (and who wouldn't): "that I had much myryer company / At the taverne than in this place" (1230–31). One really
suspects Humanyte would rather keep on sleeping, however, than go
to the tavern:

> By my troth, I care not gretely,
> For I am indyfferent to all company
> Whether it be here or there.

(1236–38)

This resumption of the merry life probably appeals to an uncultured
audience if only because it shows Humanyte sounding like a normal
human being who mouths a bit of popular philosophy and folk
psychology between drinks.

Both of Humanyte's rejections of Appetyte's influence and resump-
tions of his studies also occur with little motivation. In his first
repentance, naive Humanyte is apparently awestruck at meeting Experyence, about whom he has heard so much, and that alone is
enough to make him a scholar again (981–83). Humanyte simply
asks Appetyte to leave and does not share the latter's concern that
supper is ready and that his old company awaits him, for "Yt is but
a taverne matter" (1023). The second repentance scene, of which
only the beginning survives, commences with Nature's sudden appearance, like a *deus ex machina*, and Humanyte's lame excuse that he
has "done nothynge / That shold be contrary to your pleasynge, /
Nor never was myne intent" (1423–25). In an ironic attempt to
justify his behavior, Humanyte reminds Nature of his advice to him
to learn through his senses (289–302), but it is obvious he has misunderstood Nature's intention. Nature starts the process of correction
when the play breaks off. Humanyte would be more convincing and
certainly more dramatic if he were less passive and had greater motivation, but Rastell is uninterested in developing him as a strong-willed
character. He is merely using Humanyte's inconsistent, somewhat
comic, behavior to illustrate his theme about achieving a balance be-

tween the life of body and mind and to provide "recesses" between his "lessons."

Rastell's Taverner, however, is more interesting. Unfortunately, he does not have an appropriate name, for it might have made a more concrete impression, just as names might have rounded off the performances of A and B in *Fulgens.* Yet the lack of a name does not prevent one from appreciating Rastell's portrait of the Taverner, a well-conceived, highly comic character. As for his appearance, Appetyte's dry response to the Taverner's enthusiasm for drink indicates he has the tippler's complexion and a bulbous nose. Appropriately costumed and of customary rotundity, he has a taverner's typical vices. For example, he hesitates to rouse himself to business until he is convinced of the advantages to be gained (548–55). The Taverner's probable obesity, clumsiness, and haste must have provided a most comic display as he stumbled through the press to the stage.

Appetyte soon discovers the Taverner has another vice of that brotherhood. "I wot thou art not without good wine," Appetyte observes with sarcasm, after the Taverner praises his "new made clary" which will make anyone "By Goggys body stark madde!" (565–69). The Taverner's idea of "new wyne" is hardly a gourmet's; and, in his eagerness to please, he discloses another shady practice of his profession:

> Ye shall have wyne as newe as can be,
> For I may tell you in pryvyte
> Hit was brued but yester nyght.
>
> (917–19)

Like some taverners, he knows how to tell jokes, especially dirty ones. A call for "lyght" meat gives rise to a crack about a woman's tongue, and Humanyte's request for a stewed hen elicits the expected pun on stews (580–86). Similarly, Appetyte's request for rose water reminds the Taverner of Rose, "a fayre wench" who "dystylleth a quarte every day" (950–51). The Taverner may have offered this bawdy bit in a vengeful spirit, since Humanyte insultingly refuses his typically patronizing request for payment. The Taverner, however, can turn off sweet talk at will and turn on smart talk and insults as well as take them (937–39). His habitual mode is jovially licentious. He quickly forgets the insult and, going off to prepare Humanyte's feast, is in ecstasy at the thought of Rose:

> Yet I had lever she and I
> Where both togyther secretly
> In some corner in the spence.
>
> (955–57)

Finally, his confusion over the meaning of "thre course" and his proffered menu of a "dyshe of dreggys, a dyshe of brane, / A dysshe of draffe" (609–10) would be expected from a basically boorish, un-educated type unfamiliar with fine points of cookery. Probably both lower- and higher-class members of Rastell's audience appreciated this scene and others involving him, for the Taverner's character is fully developed, and his humor appeals to all.

Appetyte's function goes beyond that of tempter, antagonist, and allegorical opposite of the intellectual virtues. Like the "vices" of earlier and subsequent drama, and specifically like Sensualyte in *Nature* and A and B in *Fulgens*, Appetyte also performs as the chief funmaker or clown, witty servant, and parasite, the presenter of auxiliary action, like singing and dancing, as well as a performer in those entertainments. Like his forebears, he is the play's most dramatically dynamic figure.

He first appears in an ebullient mood, entering with a Wellerism: "Well hyet, quod Hykman, when that he smot / Hys wyffe on the buttockys with a bere pott" (405–6), verbally insulting Studyous, and singing catches from popular songs. "I speke as I thynke" (426), he says, making the requisite moral point, labeling himself for what he is, and beginning to tempt Humanyte by deceptively insisting on his plain-spoken honesty. Given in a solemn tone, his mock blessing of Studyous further exhibits his variety and indicates a clever change of pace. Appetyte also displays his argumentative talents early in the performance. He calls Studyous a knave; and, when Studyous returns the insult, he turns self-righteous, appealing to the audience to note how he has been insulted (444–46).

He begins his first argument in his favor in the same way Sensualyte begins his in *Nature*. To Humanyte, he says: "... I am for you so necessary / Ye can not lyve without me" (451–52). In moderate terms, he explains how "I comforte the wytts fyve" (456). But, after Humanyte asks Studyous to leave, Appetyte begins to sound more sinister and urges Humanyte to "ever study pryncypall / For to comfort your lyfe naturall" (510–11). To seal the bargain of Humanyte's lapse into "sin," Appetyte arranges for feasting and wenching. As factotum and parasitical servant, he knows where to find the tavern, how to arouse the Taverner, and how to arrange for drink, food, song, dance, and wenches for Humanyte.

Appetyte's bored, ironic responses to the Taverner's malpractices are reflected verbally in his reaction to the Taverner's joke about "stewes": "Ye, syr, it is a felow that never faylys" (588), and then he makes his own equally bad pun. A later scene matches Appetyte well with the foul-mouthed Taverner when he suggests a pint of Rose's water be poured on the Taverner's head for his ill manners (954).

Thus Appetyte, a ready wit, is apparently nobody's fool, unless his spelling talents can be construed as stupidity beneath a worldly-wise exterior (1000–1009). In this regard, some credence has to be given to Experyence's analysis of Appetyte who "nought canst nor nought wylt lere" (991). The portrayal of Appetyte as a stupid person seems to have been Rastell's idea, although he may be thinking of Medwall's Pryde, closely associated with Sensualyte in *Nature* and similarly dull beneath a glittering appearance. At Yngnoraunce's first appearance, it is hard to say whether he or Appetyte is the more stupid. Yngnoraunce stumbles over multisyllablic words, like "loso-phers" and "extromers," and boasts, in telling bit of satire, that

> I have servauntes at my retynew
> That longe to me, I assure you,
> Here within Ynglande,
> That with me, Yngnoraunce, dwell styll
> And terme of lyfe countynew wyll
> Above fyve hundred thowsand.
>
> (1145–50)

However, for the most part—and consistently with his allegorical name—Appetyte acts as Humanyte's servant, though his foolish behavior seems inappropriate for one who holds his own with a worldly-wise Taverner and bests Studyous and Experyence in the contest for Humanyte. Perhaps Yngnoraunce could have performed more appropriately when Appetyte occasionally seems so clownish. In his first appearance, Yngnoraunce displays the wit earlier associated with Appetyte and does not live up to his name's allegorical promise. In the second temptation of Humanyte, which both Appetyte and Yngnoraunce perform, no apparent distinction exists between them, although these similarities may be designed to heighten Humanyte's confusion. During the entertainment at the play's close, however, Yngnoraunce is back in character with his nonsense song about Robin Hood which may be a parody of the more orderly songs and dances organized by Appetyte.[16] Appetyte resumes his role of factotum, a task more appropriate to the clever Appetyte of the play's opening. Combined with his less public sensual promises for Humanyte and based upon his earlier exposition of the five senses (454–77), Appetyte introduces the coming entertainment: singing to delight the ear; dancing for the eye; meats and wine for the palate; damask water to scent the hall; and after that, for Humanyte, alone, not for the audience at large presumably—"A feyre wench nakyd in a couche" (1264). Appetyte, the "chefe mershal" of the "revellis," performs along with the dancers and singers and, when minstrels are called for, rushes off to the tavern ahead of the company, thinking he can find "one or twayne" there. He is, thus, his old self again, the servant of every sensual desire of both Humanyte and the audience.

After viewing the play's structure and some characters and what they reveal about Rastell's intentions, it becomes obvious that Rastell envisions himself primarily as a teacher who, knowing about educational psychology and steeped in humanistic traditions, realized that he should mix his instruction with delight. What better way to delight the lower-class audience than to offer them what looks like a morality play and a festival entertainment, while instructing them in science? What better way to influence the arisocratic and educated classes than by appealing to their responsibility, patriotism and nationalism, spirit of adventure, and already-cultivated desire for learning the most recent cosmological and geographical knowledge?

Aside from his use of low and slapstick comedy to attract a wider audience, Rastell anticipates in other ways his audience's expectations. His interest in the betterment of the common man causes him to appeal to them in their own terms. For example, he avoids formality, will not be dogmatic, and offers an apology:

> ...though the matter be not so well declaryd
> As a great clerke coude do, nor so substancyall,
> Yet the auctour hereof requiryth you all,
> Though he be yngnorant and can lytyll skyll,
> To regarde his only intent and good will.
>
> (10–14)

Such an apology is conventional enough, "but not an apology for lack of scientific information; and one cannot imagine More, Erasmus, or Vives pleading his ignorance in this manner."[17]

The Messengere's speech against gathering riches for their own sake is as much a song of praise for the common man and a reaffirmation of the nobility of labor as a call to the well-to-do to exercise noblesse oblige (71–77, 81–83). Rastell professes to regard the common people more highly than other learned men, who think scientific education is "matter to hye / And not mete for an audence unlernyd" (106–7), and he ridicules "clerkes" for pretending to a knowledge of God without an awareness of "vysyble thyngs inferyall." Thus, Rastell compliments his lower-class audience, places himself on their side, and reveals his concern for their intellectual improvement.

The Rastellian educational program deals with many issues bound to appeal to popular taste. To accomplish this educational improvement, Rastell recognizes that the vernacular must be used to translate significant works in foreign languages. In complaining of the paucity of learned books in English (12–42), he echoes King Alfred's lament of the clergy's ignorance[18] and goes beyond most of his fellow humanists whose concern for the vernacular and education of the masses included only the Bible.

Experyence, never conceived as part of the theological and metaphysical worlds of earlier playwrights, replaces some of the virtues found in earlier moralities,[19] and his presence testifies to Rastell's opinion of the value of practical knowledge as opposed to formal study. As an embodiment of virtue, Experyence makes a special appeal to the lower-class audience. Nothing abstract, scholarly, or snobbish about him, he is a traveler and a sailor (much like More's Hythloday), who had learned, done, and seen much. He knows how to use his "instrumentys" and can explain "straunge conclusions" so well "every rude carter shold them persayve playn" (395–97). Experyence, a tradesman and commoner, is more effective as a teacher, because common people can more readily understand his presentation of popular science, descriptions of America's wealth, and listing of unexplored lands.

This is not to say, however, that Experyence's geography lectures do not appeal to the higher-class members of Rastell's audience.[20] In his view, the commonweal's betterment could be brought about most easily by widespread instruction in geography, which would stimulate citizens to grasp the opportunities afforded by the colonization and Christianization of the New World. To accomplish these goals, Rastell must address himself to all segments of society, for enthusiastic commoners alone cannot man voyages of discovery, trade, and conversion.

Certainly, some information presented by Nature, Studyous, and Experyence was common knowledge to the educated. Rastell presented no original information or unique theories; he was merely aware of what was held to be reputable, current geographical knowledge. Hogrefe suggests, however, that many commoners and a sizeable portion of educated, influential Englishmen were strangely unaware of much current geographical fact. Even the educated clung stubbornly to outmoded theories and old texts and were hesitant to believe in the voyages of discovery.[21]

Other more universal ideas of the *Elementis* reflect Rastell's humanism and association with More's Circle. The Messengere's introduction, for instance, urges the wealthy and powerful to use their resources and influence for the commonweal's good, not for personal aggrandizement alone (50–84). This conception of the responsibilities of the rich is also the basis of the debate on true nobility in *Gentylnes* and *Fulgens*. After the Messengere has spoken of the improper use of "ryches," he exhorts the rich to concern themselves with the commonweal, to relieve the plight of the poor, and to "use good lyvynge."

In addition, the interlude is based on the traditional dichotomy of intellect and sensuality and the humanistic concept of "sin" as a violation, not of God's laws alone, but of an individual's nature and potential (211–17, 289–92). Nature urges Humanyte to let his intellect and reason guide him, and the play emphasizes Nature, the "benign and educative"[22] causal principle of creation. One step removed from God and concerned chiefly with earthly affairs, Nature encourages man to use free will and intellect and warns him to resist the importunate promptings of sensuality.

Although the play argues for a balance between mind—God's gift placing man between angels and animals—and body, it appeals to three distinct audiences, each with differing views on this much debated question. Many of their minds were conditioned to recognize the arguments on all sides of such issues. This ambivalence and multiplicity of possible views on the balance between mind and body account for much of the play's interest.

The *Elementis* also distinguishes carefully between an ideally balanced use of sensual powers and indulgence in any of passion's excesses, the seven deadly sins. Consideration of man's place in the grand scheme of things immediately follows the introduction of principles and revelation of conflict between mind and body: careful differentiation is made between the vegetative, animal, and intellectual levels of the chain of being. Rastell emphasizes the virtues of an earthly life well lived as a means of knowing God, and in his interlude he professes concern for ultimate theological questions and suggests uncontrolled sensuality and ignorance result in losing one's soul. In the *Elementis*, man's intellect, if allowed to "do his nature" (295), will discover first the essence of earthly life and proceed from that knowledge to an understanding of God (300–302).

Thus *The Four Elementis*, which utilizes basic morality play structure, combines serious, "sad mater" with comic episodes to teach primarily secular rather than theological lessons to early Tudor audiences. Even though its characters sometimes act inconsistently, and even though it lacks intense dramatic conflict, this experimental drama shows the skill with which Rastell took the familiar form of the morality and adapted it to serve his intentions. Such a bold experiment in reshaping a traditional form to hold the new materials of science and humanism could hardly be accomplished without some inconsistencies in characterization, plot, and structure. The play simultaneously indicates the direction from which the Tudor interlude had come and the direction toward which it would move. Rastell's work, therefore, stands as the only example of an educative interlude between Medwall's *Nature* and John Redford's *Wit and Science* and illustrates how the transition between moralities and interludes was made.

Calisto and Melebea

A product of Rastell's press entitled "A New Commodye In Maner of an Enterlude," *Calisto and Melebea* bears the ambiguous colophon, "Johēs rastell me imprimi fecit / Cum privilegio regali," followed by his more elaborate printing device; 1525–30 is generally accepted as the printing date.[23] Axton speculates that this enigmatic colophon "may mean that he had the actual printing done by sub-contract."[24] Nevertheless, Rastell may have compiled, collaborated, translated, or written all of it. Although the claim for his authorship is fairly strong, it is based entirely upon internal evidence and is thus inconclusive.[25]

Since external evidence placing *Calisto* in Rastell's canon is un-available, authorship problems cannot be resolved, and critics would be wiser to concern themselves with its mixture of genres. Is it a translation-synopsis of *La Celestina*, a morality play like the *Elementis*, which is sometimes called a "lecture in verse disguised as a play,"[26] or an entertainment or interlude as its title page indicates? *Calisto* is not a redaction like *Fulgens*, in which a sketchy source plot is expanded and its characters given greater depth and reality. But *Calisto's* author faithfully translates part of its source, and one wonders why the job was not finished. *Calisto* cannot be called a true morality, like *Nature* or the *Elementis*, wherein allegorical characters act out a traditional series of interrelationships and conflicts adding up to a thoroughly predictable lesson. Yet how can the translated fragment be explained if not as an exemplary story designed to illustrate the attached moral lesson? Nor is *Calisto* exactly like the typical interlude. Still, much like moralities, interludes emphasize moral lessons and employ humor for didacticism. Moralities seem to have been banquet entertainments, too; their clownish bawdiness and singing have entertainment value as does, for certain audiences, the learning, speculation, allusion, and debate found in them. *Calisto* likewise presents some humor and at least one song; and, if the title page describing it as an interlude and the informal approach to the audience are reliable indications, it may have been produced as a banquet entertainment.

Translating, compressing, and rearranging parts of the Spanish masterpiece,[27] the English adapter introduces six major characters (a reduction of the source's fourteen to a number appropriate to the casts and lengths of interludes) and traces the action through the first conflict, Celestina's proposal that Melebea give herself to Calisto. At this point, however, 919 lines into the 1,087-line play, the translation ceases. Melebea's father, Danio (named Pleberio in the source) enters, relates a dream he has just had, and interprets it, saying Calisto's desires are sinful and Melebea will be damned forever if she yields. Grateful for the warning, Melebea repents she was swayed even partially by Celestina's trickery and Calisto's laments and vows to retain her maiden chastity. In the final sixty-two lines, Danio urges "ye vyrgyns and fayre maydens all" (1039) to pray diligently "to withstand all evyll temptacions" (1044) and advises the audience to "rule theyr inferiours by such prudence, / To bryng them to vertew and dew obedyens" (1084–85).

Melebea's realization is not found in *La Celestina*. The work, however, professes to be a moral work, "composed as a reprimand to
wild lovers, who, overcome by their excessive appetite, call their ladies
God."[28] The violent ends of the lovers, bawd, and servants make
moral points; furthermore, *La Celestina*, like *Calisto*, ends with the
father preaching a sermon; as Pleberio carries in Melebea's broken
body, he laments the cruel falsity of the world, the inconstancy of
fortune, and the destructiveness of passionate, illicit love.

Approximately eight hundred of the 1,087 lines of *Calisto* are
literally translated from *La Celestina*.[29] The play's first forty-two lines,
Melebea's opening discourse on conflict in nature, are based upon, but
not translated directly from, the more detailed exposition in the
source's prologue. Melebea as expositor of the play's gist and her description of foolish lovers as part of nature's grand conflict, however, are original, as are the concluding 168 lines. Thus, within the
translation itself only seventy-eight lines are original. The English
author deals with only a small part of *La Celestina*—act 1, part of
act 2, act 4, and a few lines from the speeches in acts 5 and 6.[30]

Rosenbach argues that such brevity is *Calisto*'s virtue; its staging is
better, because it leaves out superfluous characters and condenses what
occasionally is a long-winded, not always sharply focused original.[31]
But critics have damned *Calisto*, too. For Fitzmaurice-Kelly, it is "a
wretched and lying piece of work."[32] While Rosenbach identifies some
of the educative aims of the English translator, he condemns him for
a false sense of ethics: "The murder of Celestina, the deaths of the
lovers, the failure to comply with poetic justice did not agree with
the nice sense of ethics of its rugged English author. The catastrophe
did not appeal to him—the Senecan climax was not to his taste.
Instead of the wonderful tragical ending of *Celestina*, he has given
us a poor substitute—a moral exhortation to virtue."[33] Allen also sees
the translator's values as false, for the adapter "does not scruple to
torture a non-moral work of art into an object lesson on prayer and
the duties of parents."[34]

The detractors, however, of both *La Celestina* and *Calisto* ignore
the differences between the two and place too much emphasis on their
similarities. One is a tragic, romantic novel, despite its employment of
acts and playbook positioning of names at the beginning of speeches,
and a work of complex intention. The other is a short play, "a new
commodye ... in maner of an enterlude"; its auspices, audience, and
intentions differ entirely from those of *La Celestina*.

The question of the translator's intention, however, remains. Why does he embark on what ostensibly is a translation, stop when only a fraction through it, then add a *deus ex machina* and a moral tag? Surely he cannot have believed he had captured the original's essence, nor is it plausible, as Allen suggests, that "at the end of Celestina's interview with Melebea either the patience of his piety and his powers of translation were exhausted, or he despaired of reducing the piece to the required dimensions."[35]

This translation of *La Celestina* is more frank in capturing the tone of the original's many bawdy passages than is Mabbe's version of 1631. These passages suggest its author only "tamed" the "wild-horse" structure of *La Celestina* to fit the limited cast and time of a dramatic entertainment, not its lively, sometimes seamy, tone. The author of *Calisto* was not squeamish, nor was his audience. In addition, the language of the translation is itself good poetry and shows no apparent diminution of vigor. Similarly without evidence is the judgment that the author discovered he was not going to produce a workable dramatic version of the whole *La Celestina*.

For several reasons, the moral lesson and the excerpt from *La Celestina* have an appropriate existence together. *Calisto* can possibly be seen as a synopsis of recent, popular Spanish literature and thus is properly called, on its title page, an interlude, offering to its audience sophisticated dramatic, literary, and educative entertainment. Simultaneously, however, *Calisto* has a traditional moral function and employs its translation to facilitate learning. Moral points are advanced about love and sex, good and bad qualities of women, beauty and ugliness, poverty and greed, youth and age, parenthood, prayer, work, and the state's well-being. Furthermore, the author recognizes a responsibility to the language; his translation of a famous foreign literary work, serious and educational in intention, will enrich the English language and the English people. Embodying an idea stated in the *Elementis* and some of his other works, this project would appeal to Rastell, and such a claim may support his authorship.

Indeed, *Calisto* is in some ways like a morality, although its outward appearances show evidence of little relationship to more traditional moralities. *Calisto* does not take the form of a conflict between the virtues and vices, as *Nature* or the *Elementis*, nor is it a debate, manned on both sides by near-abstractions, as *Fulgens* or *Gentylnes*. Its three-dimensional characters and action up to the closing sermon are translated from their source, whose realistic plot is far removed from allegory. *La Celestina* itself professes to be a serious moral work, offering lessons to those thoughtful enough to look: "they for whose true pleasure it is wholly framed; reject the story it selfe, as a vayne and idle subject, and gather out the pith and marrow of the matter for their owne good" (16–17). Similarly, *Calisto* has an obvious moral purpose, and its title page indicates it has "a morall conclusion and exhortacyon to vertew."

The play's incompleteness as a translation may be explained in part if the author's main purpose is assumed to be preaching a dramatic sermon. He lifted just enough characterization and action from the source to enable him to dramatize the moral about the responsibilities of parents to keep children busy and on virtuous paths. The English translation of part of *La Celestina* is thus complete in itself, if understood as an exemplum or cautionary tale; and, as a dramatized illustration of moral or ethical doctrine, *Calisto* can be called a morality play.

The differences, however, between *Calisto*, moralities, and its source must be emphasized. *Calisto* employs more lifelike characters than its predecessors among morality plays and has historical importance as marking a transition from allegory to realism. But these characters do not perform significant actions in varied conflicts; they are like numbers in a column with no meaning until Danio adds them up at the end. *Calisto* thus resembles a fable, at least in comparison to its sources. *La Celestina* also makes points about the spiritual harms lovers do to one another. Indeed, the novel's introduction calls it a "reprimand to wild lovers" and a warning against panders and parasites. But to say that is the moral substance of the story is to miss the points of character development and the various conflicts among the bawd, the servants, their wenches, and the lovers.

One indication of how *Calisto*'s author envisions his work can be noted in his assigning a song to Celestina (485 ff.), for she does not sing in the source. The only singing done there is by Sempronio and Calisto, who, in conventional fashion, sing sad love songs. *Calisto*'s author focuses on details of his source developing his moral point, and the same purpose dictates his departures from it. The English audience understood Celestina's song as a badge of evil. As if the traditional association of levity with sin is not clear enough, Celestina tells Parmeno she is anxious to get Calisto singing, too—to embroil him in his passionate excesses to force his purse to "swet" (488–92). Celestina reiterates the connection between song and evil later, when, acting out for Parmeno the delight found in recounting love's business, she notes songs are part of lovers' dalliance (574–75). Causing the virtuous Parmeno to sing underlines her powers as temptress and foreshadows his conversion from an honest servant to one who trusts "flatery shall spede" (632). It also prepares the audience to accept more willingly the change Celestina causes in Melebea, the chaste, though arrogant, virgin.

In addition to his moral, didactic intentions, *Calisto*'s author has serious critical and literary aims. He is trying to do something about the oft-repeated complaint of the humanist that not enough famous literary works in other tongues are translated into English. *La Celestina,* a "wark of connynge," is not merely another literary "toy" or "tryfell," of which, the Messengere in the *Elementis* (19–35) complains, there are too many. The prologue and final lament of Pleberio make apparent the moral seriousness of the Spanish work and clearly establish its author's humanistic bent and its appropriateness for dramatic adaptation as an interlude by a member of the More Circle.

Traditional moral plays are not solely serious lectures, however; their "sad matter" is mixed with humor, song, dance, and other entertainments. So, too, *Calisto* presents several types of entertainment to add variety to its message. Most important is the translation itself, the presentation of a currently popular Spanish work. Possibly the translator wished to introduce his audience to the work while simultaneously fulfilling his self-imposed, humanistic obligations of teaching morality, enriching the language, and satirizing sin and folly. Aside from its status as literature and didacticism, *La Celestina* is the sort of production a humanist would like, for it contains a wealth of "learned entertainment." Furthermore, its characters' complexity gives rise to many interpretations of human existence. Here is some of the intellectual delight medieval debate fostered at its finest. Thus *Calisto*'s author must have been attracted all the more to the possibilities of *La Celestina* for adaptation and dramatic presentation.

The play presents several debatelike conversations. The subtitle itself promises treatment of the good properties of women versus their vices and evil conditions. Sempronio takes the traditional antifeminist stand against the starry-eyed Calisto (159–265) who even praises his woman's fingernails. Parmeno defends joyful poverty before the cynical materialist, Celestina (535–49), and Celestina herself argues both sides of youth versus age (642–89).

Several references to blasphemies and heresies are also found.

Nothing is sophisticated about blasphemy and heresy, and religious imagery is frequently used with romantic subjects; however, some heretical comments in *Calisto* suggest a sophisticated audience. First, Calisto speaks of Melebea as greater than any heavenly delight, as a greater reward than any saints possess in seeing God (50–60). Similarly echoing the blasphemous complaints of the courtly lover is Calisto's claim he worships the goddess, Melebea: "there is no such sufferayn / In hevyn though she be in yerth" (157–58). Calisto paradoxically invokes the Christian deity's aid in bringing his lovelonging to a successful conclusion and sends off his pander Sempronio as he says:

> The myghty and perdurable God be his gyde,
> As he gydyd the thre kynges in to Bedleme
> From the est by the starr, and agayn dyd provyde
> As theyre conduct to retorn to theyre owne reame;
> So spede my Sempronio to quench the leme
> Of this fyre, which my hart doth waste and spende,
> And that I may com to my desyryd ende.
>
> (297–303)

The translator retains the allusion to Bethlehem of the original, but substitutes the spelling, "Bedleme," which in the early sixteenth century, according to the *OED*, was already being used in its modern sense. Uttered by the addlebrained lover, the wordplay is both serious and funny.

Similarly humorous is Celestina's blasphemy as she promises she will quickly carry to Calisto the glad tidings of Melebea's favor:

> And to Calisto with this gyrdle Celestina
> Shall go, and his ledy hart make hole and lyght.
> For Gabriell to Our Lady with *Ave Maria*
> Came never gladder than I shall to this knyght.
>
> (885–88)

Celestina's reference to herself as another Gabriel carrying to the virgin Calisto the promise of sexual consummation, a scene original in the English translation, is a monumental piece of impudence. Another passage having blasphemous overtones is Calisto's speech in which he refers to his passion's intensity:

> An yf the fyre of purgatory bren in such wyse,
> I had lever my spirete in brute bestes shuld be,
> Then to go thyder and than to the deyte.
>
> (133–35)

To this remark in which the ridiculous Calisto prefers metempsychosis to purgatory, Sempronio replies: "Mary, syr, that is a spyce of heryse."

In addition, the translator utilizes some passages smacking of blasphemy and heresy to inflict puns. In another departure from *La Celestina*, the author creates a double entendre. In the source, Celestina speaks of Melebea's girdle as having touched holy relics in Rome and Jerusalem. The English version becomes suggestive, leaving out the cities' names (836–38). A pun is also intended on "bead-folks" as Celestina says: "Fayr maydyn, for the mercy thou hast done to us, / This knyght and I both thy bedfolkis shall be" (893–94). The sexual implications of "mercy" are found here and elsewhere in Celestina's appeals for "pity" from Melebea for the "sick knyght." *Calisto* employs other double-meaning diction from the romances, such as "dy" (25), the "fyre" of love (124), the knight's "grevys" (293), and "pyne" (843), and the plea to the lady to give her lover "lyfe" (799).

Another sophisticated entertainment the translator finds in *La Celestina* may be referred to as intellectual allusion. Like its source, *Calisto* is executed as a courtly love story. All the conventions are there: the pining suitor, the cruel lady obviously protesting too much, the physical craving of the lovers, a host of impediments to consummation, and the consequent delays. Often associated with courtly love literature, though having its own long literary heritage, is the concept of fortune, and the play mentions fortune at least five times.

Several other intellectual references can be cited. The figure of Nature as the principle of earthly life, a motif critics have called sophisticated in its origins and auspices, is named in Melebea's opening speech. In addition, Calisto calls Melebea a gift of "dame Naturys," showing forth "the gretnes of God" (43–45). Several places allude to noted authors. Petrarch, "the poet lawreate," is mentioned at the opening in connection with the Nature figure (1–3). Melebea, who tries to account for Calisto's behavior and her own emotions, recalls Heraclitus and his theory of universal conflict and change (4–7). Danio's views on idleness may be intended to echo More's discussion of it in *Utopia*, and the mention of purgatory and the souls

of brute beasts may refer to Rastell's involvement in these issues.
Finally, references to Nimrod (164), Alexander the Great (165,
851), the liturgy of St. John's feast (171), Elias (175), Paris and
Venus (247), Hector (852), St. George (855), the "gentyll Nar-
ciso" (858), and others presuppose an audience educated enough to
appreciate them.

Averting the tragic ending of its source, this interlude substitutes
satiric comedy, its principal target being romantic love. To hit this
mark, it enlists the aid of a young, naive lover blinded to the realities
of women, love, and life; a virgin untried in the ways of the world
and prey to her "girlish" sentiments; and a seemingly "holier-than-
thou" bawd. The play, then, aims at some of the "silly" Petrarchan
conventions used by a cool lady who protests too much and a hot lover
whose many oxymorons indicate the physical, mental, and emotional
disharmony such love can cause.

Calisto's author, however, focuses these conventions on Melebea and
her assent to consummate her romance and depicts it in moral terms
as a temptation, fall, sin, examination of conscience, repentance, and
forgiveness, all of which are followed by "a moral conclusion and
exhortacyon to vertew." To manipulate audience response to these
events, Axton sees a "simple principle of dramatic construction" in
which "there are almost equal 'acts' (1–309, 310–632, 633–919)
and an epilogue (920–1087)."[36] Nevertheless, characters as foils,
foreshadowing, verbal repetitions and parallels, juxtaposition of action and speeches, materials of debate, proverbs, double entendres,
and amazingly vital language complicate this simple construction.

Axton's view of the play's characters and themes is not as simple
as that of other critics, such as Hogrefe, whose ideas about the
author, his probable auspices, and themes contain some misplaced
emphasis that need to be modified. Hogrefe believes Vives, who was
"almost fanatical" about chastity, influenced the play's composition.
If the More Circle was as fanatically opposed to romantic literature
as Vives was, *Calisto*, a straitlaced takeoff on a typically decadent
Spanish romance, presents the humanist's alternative to romantic excesses.[37] Hogrefe's argument, however, may begin with faulty prem-
ises. As a result, some of her conclusions about its moral intent, its
author's literary conception, and the More Circle are out of focus.
First, the translated portion does not differ from its source in its
presentation of passion. The one faithfully copies the other; contrary
to Hogrefe's claim, the love affair and courtly love conventions and,

most importantly, the characters of the courtly lovers are the same. The crux is Melebea's character in *Calisto*.

Far from being, in Hogrefe's words, the "ideal maiden" cruelly tricked into "wavering," Melebea knows the implications of giving Celestina the token, her "gyrdyll," and asking her to return "secretly" for the "prayer" (876–77). Melebea is intelligent. Though she has experienced little, she has read much. She quotes Heraclitus and Petrarch (1–7), and Calisto praises her "excellent wyt" (221). Melebea says, "I perseyve the entent of thy wordys all" (64), when Calisto lavishes praise upon her and reveals, in conventionally euphemistic language, he wants to go to bed with her (45–60). Celestina only mentions Calisto's name amid a flow of compliments, prayers, and non sequiturs, and Melebea catches on: "A ha! is this the entent of thy conclusyon? / Tell me no more of this matter, I charge the" (780–81) and "Thinkist thou that I understand not, thou falls mother, / Thy hurtfull message, thy fals subtell ways?" (805–6).

Melebea understands, because she knows how the game of courtly love is played. She is supposed to be cruel, to ignore her suitor's plaints, using moral or personal excuses and to protest violently—to preserve the appearance of cruelty, disdain, or virtue—when someone reveals an awareness of the affair and proposes to take part in it. (Whatever else Melebea may be called, her verbal abuse of Celestina [780–830] is proof enough that she is not the "ideal maiden.") After a decent time, should her feelings for the suitor tend that way, she is supposed to give him a token, then follow through on further arrangements.

In *La Celestina*, Melebea finally reveals her craving for Calisto to Celestina (implied by Melebea's speech [633–35] in *Calisto*, suggesting she has sought out Celestina), and the pander begins to work actively for both sides. Clearly Melebea is at first sad to see her father upset: "For I have no cause but to be mery and glad" (933), she says, and one, of course, knows why. Then Danio relates his dream. Melebea, her Christian sensibilities shocked, no longer wishes to play the game. She assures her father she did not disgrace him and confesses "though I dyd consent / In mynd, yet had he never hys intent" (1009–10). Melebea does take that first step into sin, the willing acceptance of its circumstances. The deed's consequences, which form the framework of the rest of *La Celestina*, are outside the scope and purpose of the English production. Up until the close with Danio, however, Melebea is presented exactly as she is in the source.

CARNE... ....
LIVINGSTONE COLLEGE
SALISBURY, N. C. 28144

How do these facts, then, affect Hogrefe's interpretation? Can *Calisto* be called a "deliberate piece of propaganda for the beauty and good properties of women"? The answer is yes, but some distinctions must be made. The subtitle says that *Calisto* deals with the good properties and "vycys and evyll condicions" of women. In Celestina, the bawd, one obviously sees many "vycys and evyll condicions," although she is not entirely unsympathetic, since she is old, foul, and poor (or pretending to be poor). Most of the audience probably saw her as evil, but some may have deemed her state in part due to "nede and poverte" (1073) and other social conditions the More Circle felt in need of remedy. In Melebea, the courtly lover, one also sees a few "vycys and evyll[s]," such as pride in her status and beauty, hypocrisy and game playing, and rudeness. In Melebea, the intelligent woman and devoted, repentant daughter, one sees the "bewte and good properties of women." Melebea, the heroine, is not simply the innocent wayfaring pilgrim beset by evil through no fault of her own.

Humanists in general and the More Circle in particular do not give simple answers to complex questions. They do not condemn human behavior out of hand, without simultaneously attempting to understand causes and motives. In these early humanistic plays, then, specific moral alternatives are not stated, argued for, and recommended over others. Rather, all opinions are presented simultaneously for individual consideration and judgment. Questions are asked, issues are raised, but there is little desire to rush in with dogmatic conclusions. The humanist author of *Calisto* may intend to satirize courtly love conventions and Spanish romances, while he argues seriously through Danio for prayer, reasoned behavior, and fulfilling occupation. However, another part of the humanist's point of view is an all-embracing sympathetic understanding, a willingness, as the prologue of *La Celestina* puts it, to gather, even from "vayne and idle" subjects, the "pith and marrow" of the matter for their "owne good and benefit," while laughing at "those things that savour only of wit, and pleasant conceits." A closed-mind approach to sexual behavior, for which Hogrefe suggests *Calisto*'s author is arguing, would make sheer farce of all but the play's end, and *Calisto* has much more value and depth than that.

Indebted to *La Celestina* for plot, setting, and realistic characters, *Calisto* is the first translation of an important Spanish work into English, and the Celestina story continued to be presented to English audiences throughout the sixteenth century. *Calisto* itself, absorbing

and transmitting some of the greatness of its source, is the first play
employing realistic-romantic comedy in English and "points clearly
towards the great romantic movement that some fifty years later en-
riched England and the world with its most precious dramatic master-
pieces."[38] A kind of embryonic tragicomedy, the play is distantly
related to *All's Well that Ends Well.*[39] But there is a more obvious
relationship; had *Calisto*'s author dramatized the complete source, he
might have done more in foreshadowing *Romeo and Juliet.*

To a large extent, the humanist author of *Calisto* observes traditional assumptions and methods in constructing his moral play. He
excerpts a longer work of a different genre and presents his reaction
to illustrate and dramatize a moral point. He utilizes standard humorous devices to embellish his lesson. Simultaneously, he presents entertainment over and above music and low-life humor; debate material, theological and philosophical problems, and intellectual allu-
sions—all are embodied in a preview and perhaps a satire of a currently popular, foreign literary work. However, these similarities to
moral plays, like *Nature* and the *Elementis*, and to interludes, like
Fulgens, should not obscure what is original and potentially influential
in *Calisto*. Although its virtues are largely those of its source, in the
context of English drama in the first third of the sixteenth century,
the play uniquely foreshadows important dramatic developments.

Of Gentylnes and Nobylyte

Of Gentylnes and Nobylyte, chiefly a debate on the definition of
a gentleman, the concept of nobility, and the qualifications of rulers,[40]
is called a "dyalogue" on its title page. It employs three interlocutors:
a Knyght, a Marchaunt, and a Plowman. For the first 174 lines, the
Knyght and Marchaunt argue their respective classes are more gentle-
manly and most worthy to rule. But these representatives of the social
structure join forces against the Plowman, whose rival definitions of
and claims to nobility and whose volatile criticisms of the ruling
classes determine the play's direction and content. In an epilogue, the
Phylosopher summarizes the main points and urges rulers to live up
to their responsibilities.

Each part is divided in the middle by comic brawls. The first fight
commences at the Plowman's entrance (174) and follows the opening debate between the Knyght and Marchaunt; the second bout
comes halfway through the argument on inheritance and related is-

sues (714). The sequence of ideas throughout is natural and inevitable enough, but non sequiturs and irrelevancies exist as they might in any argument. The debate as such, then, is realistic; in the sense it is put on in prearranged terms by actors before an audience, it is dramatic, too. While debates perform secondary dramatic functions in *Calisto*, the debate is almost the total substance of *Gentylnes*. Such a lack of plot in the traditional sense is irrelevant, since depth of characterization goes a long way toward providing dramatic entertainment.

The authorship of *Gentylnes* continues to be debated, and proponents of both Rastell and Heywood join the issue. Supporters of Rastell's authorship rely heavily on thematic arguments, seeing it as yet another document in his program of ideas for the betterment of mankind and the state. In fact, if the Plowman's arguments about the importance of "naturall reason" and other topics are heard as Rastell's voice, the play's structure may reflect his authorship. Indeed, the Plowman speaks almost twice as many lines as the Knyght and Marchaunt (527 to the Knyght's 300 and Marchaunt's 272). Only the Phylosopher holds the stage alone for more time than the Plowman. Not only his verbal presence, but also his physical forcefulness, implied in his entrance "with a short whyp in hys hand" and made explicit in his tendency to initiate fights, lend credence to Rastell's authorship.[41]

Heywood's supporters[42] emphasize similarities between *Gentylnes* and Heywood's plays—skillfully constructed dialogue-debate, lifelike characterization, humor, and polished verse—and agree the *Elementis*, supposedly poor by comparison—could not have the same author as *Gentylnes*. Most commentators overlook the possibilities of collaboration and revision. Axton agrees with Cameron's cautious conclusion that Heywood wrote most of the play and Rastell the epilogue and adds a new dimension to it. To advance the theory of collaboration, he points to the mixture of Latin and English stage directions and "the possibility of some actual social rivalry between 'gentylman' Heywood and his father-in-law."[43]

On the other hand, the case for Heywood, although based on apparently objective criteria, is not as strong as it first appears. Bevington offers telling arguments against Heywood's authorship. Even though he prefaces his remarks by saying that "joint authorship is by no means out of the question," his analysis of the dramatic viewpoint and tone of *Gentylnes* points to Rastell as author. Briefly, Bevington contends that *Gentlynes* is more "down-right," more "preachy" than Heywood's known plays, and that the politically radical themes introduced by the Plowman have the blessings of the author, a serious, blunt, outspoken humanist concerned with the foibles of humankind and abuses within the establishment. Such an author, Bevington contends, Heywood is not.[44]

As with *Calisto*, there is little external evidence to support internal conjectures about authorship. Its colophon—"Johēs rastell me fieri fecit"—is too ambiguous to prove authorship; it may merely refer to Rastell as publisher-printer. But that Rastell did not name his son-in-law if Heywood was indeed the author is unusual. Yet the same woodcut of Heywood that prefaces the editions of *The Spider and the Fly* prefaces some editions of the play. What becomes obvious is that only tentative comments can be made about authorship: it could be entirely Rastell or Heywood's, a collaboration or revision between them, or neither may have composed it.

The play opens with the Marchaunt's boasts about his contribution to the commonwealth. The Knyght joins him, and their arguments concern true nobility. The Knyght lists his criteria for a gentleman: "Mary, I call them gentlymen that be / Born to grete landys by inherytaunce" (30–31). The Marchaunt counters with this argument,

> For I call hym a gentylman that gentilly
> Doth gyf unto other men lovyngly
> Such thing as he hath of hys own proper.
>
> (45–47)

The Knyght then argues his ancestors were wiser than the Marchaunt's, a claim the Marchaunt quickly denies. The Knyght boasts of wise judges and courageous warriors; the Marchaunt brags of skillful artisans. Bursting with pride, the Knyght sums up his argument, not knowing the Plowman, the third disputant, is listening. The technique of sharply penetrating characters' pretensions and blind spots through comic contrast is evident (171–78). When the Plowman attacks the assumption that nobility results from ancestry, he echoes the thinking of the More Circle on true nobility: "And of the actys that your ancestours did before / Ye are the nobler never the more" (220–21).

Having declared the dispute of the Knyght and Marchaunt worthless because they superficially tout the accomplishments of their ancestors and not their own, the Plowman begins to prove his claim to nobility. The two who were arguing against each other's claims now appear to side together as they list their personal services to the realm in an attempt to appease the Plowman. He, however, has his own case to make, and asks,

> Is not that the noblyst thyng in dede
> That of all other thyngis hath lest nede,
> As God which reynith etern in blysse?

(281–83)

When they agree no reasonable man can deny this truth, the Plowman, by false analogy, draws this conclusion: "So, suffycency is ever noblenes, / And necessyte is ever wrechydnes" (295–96). Since he plows, "tyll[s]," makes the "corn to habounde," nourishes the "catell and fowlys . . . fyssh and herbis" (309–14), and supplies all his needs—while they depend on him to supply theirs—he is "more noble than" (340) either of them.

In anger, the Marchaunt lashes back with an exaggerated consequence of the Plowman's reasoning:

> . . . thou woldyst have
> Everi best, fyssh, and other foule than
> To be more noble of birth than a man.
> For man hath more nede of bodely coveryng
> Than they have, for they nede no thynge.

(342–46)

Here the Plowman discourses on man's rational soul which more than supplies the defects of his body and insures his superiority over animals. The Marchaunt, realizing that he is defeated, declares this point a digression and insists that they return to the original subject: "Which was to prove who was the most gentylman, / Whych we disputyd. I wold thou haddist hard it" (400–401).

In the first part, then, two commonplace Tudor ideas are explored "in maner of an enterlude with divers toys and gestis addyd therto to make mery pastyme and disport": the relationship between birth and true nobility and the superiority of man's soul. These arguments on social and moral questions are presented through definitions, generalizations, and exempla, and are agreed upon or disputed in dramatic deliveries complete with costumes, gestures, and some action. Often exaggerated for comic effects in order to "defuse" potentially radical, explosively serious social, moral criticism, such arguments are stated in plain, colloquial language containing understatements and over-statements, proverbs, and syllogisms. Some members of Tudor audiences were familiar with most of these viewpoints and devices, so the play probably caused them to think further and question what they knew, because more is concerned "with what can be said on each side than with the strict logic of what is said."[45]

When the Plowman excuses himself to "by . . . a halporth of gresse" (405), the pause allows for some lighter entertainment before the three disputants debate the more serious question around which the second half centers: do gentleness and nobility consist of ancestry, inheritance, and property or virtuous conditions alone? As expected, the Plowman argues from man's common parentage in Adam and Eve, reiterating the old saw, "For when Adam dolf and Eve span, / Who was then a gentylman?" (485–86). To him, noble birth does not exist. In retaliation, the Knyght traces the rise of his ancestors to noble status. Once, he says, "ther were but few people" (572), so "All thyng was in commyn" (575). "When people dyd increse" (576), "grete strf and debate dyd aryse" (579) over possessions. Then the Knyght's ancestors formulated "laws" in order "the people myght be / Lyffng togedyr in pease and unyte" (581–82). At first, those under his ancestors gave goods for these "laws," later "money an annyell rent" (592).

The Plowman's historical perspective (597–602), however, differs vastly, and he counters the Knyght's claims that much good comes from inheritance (646–58). To change a subject becoming painful to him, the Knyght asks what the Plowman thinks of merchants, and the Plowman launches his attack against corrupt merchants, though admitting many are virtuous and just. Here the Knyght demonstrates the action has moved, in a way, from the stage to a lecture room, in which certain topics must be discussed. Finally, the Knyght can no longer control his anger; the Marchaunt must prevent a fight between him and the Plowman. This abortive, comic struggle, a repetition of the fisticuffs in part 1 and another indication of stage action, offers a welcome break in the argument and provides an abrupt, but effective transition to the next question about the value of inheritance.

The Knyght believes inherited lands and titles promote "all good rule and ordynaunce" (768), while the Plowman maintains that they are the source of social, economic, and legal injustice. He then advances his own solution to the problem: there should be no inheritance, and only rulers should possess property; those who think only of their descendents should not be allowed to rule or to hold land. Furthermore, estates should only be held for the term of the owner's life (776–78). Thus, the Plowman proposes some of the same ideas about communal property and the obligation to work for the commonweal's good that More expresses in *Utopia*. Once again, he declares one possesses the quality of nobleness, because of "gentyll condycions" (866), not inheritance.

The Marchaunt insists on returning to the original subject, but the disputants are unable to reach any solution. The Plowman, alone on stage briefly before the others reenter and unable to see his own blindness on some issues, speaks directly to the audience, ironically commenting on the self-interest of all and placing little hope in man's abilities to resolve such questions through reason. Tired, he sees the "amendement of the world is not" (1004) in him, so he "wyll let the world wagg" (1010), go home, "dryf the plowgh" (1011), and pray

> . . . . God wyl send
> A tyme tyll our governours may intend
> Of all enormytees the reformacyon,
> And bryng in thyr handis the rod of correccyon,
> And the reformyng of injuryes them self see,
> And wyll sey precysely, "thus it shall be."
>
> (996–1001)

Ironically, as if to underline the Plowman's expression of his lack of hope in changing man's ideas and ways, the Knyght and Marchaunt enter to disparge their opponent smugly and present the advantages of inherited rule safely. They can agree they are superior to the Plowman, so they do not renew their original argument. The play seems complete when the two disputants leave the stage, but an unannounced Phylosopher enters to deliver a lengthy, didactic epilogue. The Phylosopher announces that the actual criterion for gentility

> Ys but vertew and gentyl condycyons,
> Whych as well in pore men oft tymes we se
> As in men of grete byrth or hye degre.
>
> (1109–11)

Briefly discussing nobility, he agrees with the Plowman that it consists partially, but not entirely, of self-sufficiency, He continues and corrects the Plowman's false analogy between self-sufficiency in God and man. Not only for His self-sufficiency, but also for His goodness, is God God. So, man's imitation of such goodness "is ever the thyng pryncypall / That gentlynes and noblenes doth insue" (1121–22), and only those who possess it should rule. Finally, he comments upon how man can become more noble and upon "who shuld be chose to hye auctoryte" (1104). Ever qualifying what he says with realizations of man's inherent weakness, he makes practical suggestions for achieving these ideals; and, as Altman says: "in the end, then, he does have a plan for making things better. He does not advocate abolition of inheritance and the public ownership of land, nor does he share the Plowman's pessimism about the use of reason to effect change; yet he has adapted the concepts of rotation of appointed officials and their liability to the public. In effect, he presents a meliorist view of the important questions raised in the dialogue."[46] Altman's position, however, sounds more optimistic than that of the Phylosopher. Though the Phylosopher believes in the efficacy of his ideas for reform, he little hopes to see them in practice and prays "God of his grace . . . / To reforme shortly such thynges amys" (1168–69).

The themes of *Gentylnes* have sometimes been misread, because the characters of the Knyght, Marchaunt, and especially the Plowman have been read in two-dimensional terms. The Phylosopher clearly makes the point that "these reasons here brought in" are "Both agayns men of hye and of low degre" (1129–30). A sympathetic reading shows that one cannot regard the Plowman, for example, as its moral center, as Hogrefe and Bevington suggest,[47] for his faults and foolishness loom too large. He does possess some learning and common sense, but the truth he utters is colored by his probably courtly audience, by his bad manners, conceit, and boorish self-righteousness— all creating the dominant flavor of high comedy that is so much a part of *Gentylnes*. The play's humor makes it difficult to argue that the author intended to support any particular school of thought or political position. The answers *Gentylnes* provides for the world's problems—if they are provided at all—are not so easy to pin down.

Its humor is found primarily in the Plowman's personality: a unique combination of innate good sense, intellectual perception, insight into human nature, and particularly human foibles, all mixed with a measure of an arrogant, abusive, and ill-mannered tongue;

pretensions to wisdom; and a boastful complacency simultaneously making him believe farm life is for all and imbuing him with a certain provinciality. The Plowman does occasionally make sense, and he reveals a certain incisiveness of mind. While not formally educated, he has thought about human problems and is able to detect folly in others. At times a painfully honest, Christian moralist who is quick to blast the pretentions and exploitations of knights, clergy, merchants, and others, the provincial, proverbial Plowman can also be an almost villainous satirist, ill-mannered fool, and bully at other times.[48]

Like the Plowman, both the Knyght and Marchaunt provide humor by displaying their inconsistencies, foibles, and the vices of each of their classes, while also making occasionally sensible contributions. Critics are wrong to write off the Knyght and Marchaunt as a pair of latter-day vices.[49] As with the Plowman, to understand the Knyght and Marchaunt is to be aware that their moral posture and the play's are not readily definable. To appreciate the depth of their natures is to realize that the author, both a playwright and a humanist teacher, is not crude or simpleminded.

Both the Knyght and Marchaunt make some valid points in the debate on gentility, sufficiency, inheritance, and fitness to rule. They are not totally foolish or vicious men, any more than the Plowman is. Fittingly enough, the Marchaunt reveals a shrewd practicality as he tries to keep the conversations to the point and as he discovers errors in the Plowman's reasoning. Both men are able to hold their own with the clever Plowman, although he determines the discussion's flow and thus commands a greater share of the spotlight. Although they join against the Plowman, the Knyght and Marchaunt are carefully differentiated as types of their classes. The personalities which emerge are not attractive; but, as with the Plowman, the voices of the Knyght and Marchaunt serve to balance and qualify the truths or apparent truths they present, while simultaneously creating the all-embracing high comic atmosphere of *Gentylnes*.

The Knyght has the stock characteristics of the aristocrat satirized in comedy. Pompously solemn, he is given to rhetorical boasting of his ancestors and martial prowess. The Knyght is not completely without intellectual capacities, for he does make reasonable, incisive comments in several exchanges with the Marchaunt and Plowman. However, several remarks hint he is, appropriately enough, a little dull, since he argues from limited experience and complacent self-interest. The Knyght's typical demeanor toward his inferiors is over-bearing and disdainful. In troubled circumstances, his hot temper quickly gives rise to invective, and his insults cause the first conflict with the Plowman. In part 2, when all three characters, but especially the Knyght, gradually lose control of themselves and start fighting anew, his insults are the proximate cause of that battle, too. Such qualities render his defense of his estate and inheritance (because they preserve law and order, education and other "gentyl condycons") all the more ironic.

The Marchaunt's character is also worked out in depth. As one of the rising bourgeoisie, he has the vices peculiar to that class. In the opening lines, for example, he takes the simple economic fact that commerce benefits the commonwealth, overstates its implications, glosses over his real motives, and draws a questionable conclusion about his nobility (1–10). The Marchaunt may be clever and worldly-wise, but he has the blunted sophistication and aesthetic sense of typical nouveau riche. He believes he is a true gentleman, because his forebears, tradesmen and artisans, helped the Knyght's ancestors (61–62). For him, nobility derives from wit, defined simply as performing a trade skillfully.

Once the Plowman injects his forceful personality into the scene, the Marchaunt is forced to ally himself with the Knyght, an arrangement which gave the former, if not the latter, great satisfaction. He sees his spurious arguments for his nobility failed to convince the Knyght, and he must have realized why: no amount of money can buy an aristocratic family tradition which has ever been understood as a *sine qua non* of nobility. Thus, the Marchaunt becomes a servile flatterer, curries the Knyght's favor by mouth, and ingratiates himself into the aristocracy. His obsequiousness, raised to burlesque proportions, must have occasioned the audience's laughter. One device is largely responsible for this humor: the loud-mouthed, social-climbing Marchaunt presumes to speak for the Knyght, the aristocratic audience, and the Plowman's betters in general. The Knyght is either too upset by or preoccupied with the iconoclastic, disrespectful Plowman to realize what the Marchaunt is doing or too confident of his own worth and too scornful of the Marchaunt's to care. The Marchaunt must have been wary of his presumption at first, but he is gratified that the Knyght does not put him down and becomes increasingly intoxicated with his counterfeit sense of importance. Consequently, the Marchaunt speaks almost solely for upper-class prerogatives, and one could contemplate the ironies implicit in his use of "we."

Finally, a word should be said about the Marchaunt's role in the two sets of fisticuffs. In all likelihood, he is not a party to the fighting that twice erupts. The stage directions *"Et verberat eos"* ("And he beats them") and *"Et hic verberat eos"* ("And here he beats them") probably refer only to the Plowman and Knyght, since they are the last to speak before the fights begin and clearly threaten one another (192 ff., 714 ff.). To fail to see the Marchaunt as a noncombatant and peacemaker is to miss his character's nuances. The Marchaunt—the shrewd, crafty, overweight, physically graceless, and less-than-honest entrepreneur, trying to climb the social ladder, and in all likelihood presented as overdressed in finery by virtue of his newfound luxury—deliberately stays out of combat. It is unclear whether he acts because of cowardice, because he is more cool-headed than the Knyght, or because he is too politic and practical to do or say anything that may be to his immediate or future disadvantage.

Considering all facets of their personalities, suggesting the Knyght, Marchaunt, and Plowman merely stand for their estates or conflicting sides in existing social, economic, or political structures is simplistic. The perceptive humanist audience probably did not regard the Plowman's conflict with the Knyght as revolutionary in its implications, for the Knyght is not that admirable a representative of his class. He is a satirical figure, an appropriate butt of verbal and slapstick abuse by reason of his pompous bombast. Since his faults are obvious, the aristocratic audience was not likely to identify too closely with him or to take as reflections upon themselves the Plowman's attacks. The Marchaunt berates the Plowman for "dysturb[ing] all thys hole company" (717), but is speaking as a sycophant and social climber, seeing his own faults exposed and his would-be status undermined by the Plowman. The Plowman, whose blind spots are evident enough, knows the audience: "Nay, mary, it is a cause to make them mery, / To walke such a proude foole is but sport and game" (718–19). The Knyght has proved himself as a "proude foole," and experience sanctions his fate at the Plowman's hands.

It seems, then, that one would be hard put to describe the play in simplistic terms or to posit a political, social, educational, or moral dichotomy between the farmer and richer men. The play is simple in its thematic intention, but its simplicity can be understood only if one perceives the complex artistic ramifications of the debate, the intellectual and humorous appeals made to a sophisticated audience, and the correspondences of these ramifications to realities behind human and worldly appearances as understood by men who think deeply. To note minor points of the debate or a series of specific issues is certainly helpful in understanding its fullness, but to concentrate on them is to overlook the largest, most basic implication of *Gentylnes* and can thus be misleading, suggesting a play of more universal intention is narrowly topical or argumentative. Perhaps focusing on topical references and commonplaces is not as important as appreciating its overall effect, which is what interests one over four hundred years and was possibly the main concern of its humanist author also.

Gentylnes is unlike other plays of the More Circle in that it mainly teaches, argues for, and illustrates general principles rather than specific solutions. The humanist understands the complexity of the human condition. In any situation, multiple and simultaneous interpretations are the rule, despite the simplistic arguments of moralists and politicians who, by preaching and legislating, force reality to conform to their understanding of it. Even apparently sensible opinions and judgments are in life colored, distorted, and brought into question by human selfishness and the consequent inability to know and speak the whole truth. This inability must, for the thinking man, raise questions about the value of any judgment or opinion. The Phylosopher's epilogue sums up the general areas on which all reasonable men can agree. Indeed, the three interlocutors of the play would deny none of it.[50] In *Gentylnes*, some "radical ideas are expressed," writes Altman,

with no expectation that they will be adopted, but the two sides shape together some more immediately realizable goal. The result is two-fold: an acceptable *via media* is reached by which the general state of things is improved because the most reasonable elements on both sides are embraced; at the same time, what has been said in behalf of both extremes remains in the mind to stir further thought. In intellectual and political terms, this describes a process of debate and compromise, in which the ideas temporarily discarded are shelved for use at a more appropriate time. In literary terms, it describes an antithetical drama whose contrary elements reach a tentative equilibrium, but are always ready to settle out again.[51]

On the other hand, there is much truth in the Plowman's final assertion that, in the long run, not a great deal can be done about human problems:

> ... all the grete argumentes that we thre
> Have made syth we resonyd here togedyr
> Do not prevayle the weyght of a fether
> For the helpyng of any thyng that is amys.
>
> (1005–8)

Certainly, the debate verifies that none of its participants has changed his views, despite the varying viewpoints to which each has been exposed. When the personalities of the three speakers are allowed to influence their reasoning together, the result, if not falsehood, is half-truth, oversimplification, and the consequent weakening of the bonds of love, sympathy, and mutual understanding. Implicitly, the Plowman's statement confirms the humanists' belief that, through the use of reason, man can be persuaded to decisive action capable of producing change. Couple with this the tendency of all to flaunt their own virtues and those of their estates and ignore their weaknesses, and one has revealed a damning indictment of human nature and a perennially relevant explanation of man's failure to progress. Troubles in human relations arise not when one or another political or class system is followed, but when that system is imposed and made to function with hostility, suspicion, and selfishness.

Gentylnes, then, is the literary embodiment of these moral attitudes of the humanists. The debate reveals the common ground of humanistic good sense all men can readily share, while it illustrates precisely how human personalities with all their faults can subvert that common body of knowledge, the individual's own otherwise sound judgments, and the state's order. The brawls between the Plowman and Knyght have symbolic, educative value and are thus more than mere comic relief. *Gentylnes* demonstrates why human institutions are by definition imperfect and impermanent. The play illustrates the attitude central to the humanist faith in man: it is not as important to provide answers as it is to be certain that the right questions are asked. Thus, *Gentylnes* is a synthetic model of reality as the humanist understands it and herein lies its most significant theme and the key to understanding its method.

Chapter Three
The Prose Works

Two prose works, *The pastyme of people* and *A new boke of Purgatory*, manifest the restless, inquisitive nature of Rastell, who became a member of Parliament in 1529. Active in too many areas of endeavor at once, Rastell repeats his familiar pattern. As with most of his earlier projects, neither of his prose works is totally successful. Yet each attests to the earnestness of his motives as a printer-historian-propagandist who, seeing an ill in his society, seeks to remedy it by the use of his pen and printing press. Thus, the redeeming feature of each of these works, though abundant with mundane and didactic sections, is the insight each offers into the thought of an overly zealous, active Tudor citizen with pretensions to humanism.

The pastyme of people

As if determined to prove his versatility, the indomitable Rastell turned to yet another project, a history. An interest in the humanist revival of history writing, the development of his activities as a legal antiquary, or the continuing desire to prove himself an equal of his kinsman, More, and his Circle may have motivated his move to this new field.

Rastell probably compiled his history in 1529, the year of its publication. The use of his apprentices to assemble sections of the history and oversee its printing[1] may explain the failure of this book to meet the standards Rastell set for other works from his press. The size of its printing is unknown, but copies soon became scarce and only one perfect copy is extant.[2] That the history has survived to reach a larger audience is due to the work of T. F. Dibdin, who reprinted it in 1811.[3] Despite his interest in Rastell's work, Dibdin could not refrain from criticizing it. His target was its printing, which he considered "barbarous"; in fact, Dibdin declares it impossible to imagine a book "more rudely printed" (vi). Other critics complain that the parallel column arrangement of the histories of England and other sections of Europe is confusing, sometimes scattering the treatment of a particular country throughout.[4] Rastell chose this method to present differing opinions of an event on the same page, but the result often proves counterproductive. Also deplored is the use of printer's ornaments to fill up lines and mark divisions; this expedient gives the printing "an unsightly appearance."[5]

One aspect of *The pastyme* which interests students of printing is its use of woodcuts to portray prominent historical and religious figures. No one knows who executed these woodcuts, although Holbein has been suggested.[6] That Rastell might have ventured into this artistic endeavor is not inconceivable. After all, he had designed decorations for the banquet hall at the Field of the Cloth of Gold and the extravaganza staged at Greenwich in 1527.[7] If he did try wood engraving, the results, which some authorities term "boldly conceived" and "not without merit" considering "the wretched state of wood carving in England at that time,"[8] are as significant as his contributions to the printing of music.[9] Of all the illustrations, those of the kings of England from William I to Richard III hold the most interest. Rastell used these woodcuts to illustrate a moral judgment upon each king. For rulers whose reigns saw civil war and rebellion, he depicts their scepters bent down, upside down, or broken. Those rulers whose reigns brought external warfare carry swords and orbs and appear in armor and robes.

These woodcuts as well as the parallel columns serve to illustrate one of Rastell's motives in producing a history. His cause is the education of the English people; his method employs the woodcuts for didactic moralizing to instill virtue and goodness in readers. This humanistic goal, pervading all Rastell undertook, remained the guiding principle of his life; but however sincerely he adopted the humanist ideals, they nevertheless were adopted and not original. Though on the periphery of the humanist circle surrounding his brother-in-law, Rastell was willing to put the ideas of his more gifted contemporaries into print. While not unaware of the pecuniary advantages of printing, he believed in its power to influence his fellow citizens. As he explains in *The pastyme*, printing "hathe ban cause of great lernynge and knowelege, and hathe ben the cause of many thyngs and great chaunges" (269).

Change was a common tenet of the humanists, although methods and degrees were not agreed upon. In general, they felt that all areas of life deserved an examination and that needed changes and improvements might thereby be ascertained and executed by enlightened rulers and judicious civil servants. In politics, the emphasis was not upon God's vengeance on sinful man but on those political and social conditions capable of being changed by man's will. By using this approach, Rastell could justify the importance of history for understanding the human condition. This emphasis upon man in his world should not be interpreted as deemphasizing the role of Providence in human affairs; indeed, Rastell's printer's device illustrates the belief that an ominiscient God observes all things. But the shift from the history of God's intervention in man's actions to the history of man's actions placed God in the position not of prime mover but of divine observer who seldom interrupted.

As a consequence, history became for the Tudor humanists an urgent means for man to comprehend his place in a world directly evidencing the follies or triumphs of past human endeavor. Little effort was made to develop theories of historiography or define a philosophy of history. The humanists exhibited a "profoundly utilitarian bent," claims Arthur B. Ferguson,[10] in their use of history for didactic purposes. Combining this conviction with the ideal of the active, educated citizen, they concluded that history should be popularized and supplied to those classes outside the scholarly circle. To fulfill this obligation to his fellowmen became "one of the self-imposed duties of a humanist"[11] like Rastell.

Rastell used as his sources both chronicles and histories, the legacies of the medieval period popularized through the printing press. From these, in the fashion of his time, he compiled *The pastyme*. If his work has merit for students of Tudor times, it is in the way Rastell adapted the material of his sources to his purposes. As a humanist-historian, he merits little distinction; but as an educated man, his interest in the past and view of the historical process deserve consideration. His narrative is not inspired, but neither were his sources. Indeed, traditions and legends which discouraged originality shackled Rastell.[12] That he managed to overcome some hinderances makes his effort unique.

The compulsion of previous writers to trace British ancestry to famous men of the past confronted the historian-patriot.[13] Throughout the medieval age, chroniclers sought to find lists of dynasties to prove English rulers descended from an Aeneas or a Japheth. Britain had to have as its founder a warrior-hero. Absent in the work of these chroniclers was concern for the truth of prehistoric times; to them, the first chapters of man's existence were unimportant because, regardless of events, God was present. Since the medieval writer felt his purpose to be the description of God's influence on man's affairs, he considered it proper to depict the past in an appealing light before hastening on to describe God's role in present times.

Within these confines for framing history, several traditions about the beginning of England developed. One of the most attractive stories featured a Trojan prince, Brutus, who founded Britain in heroic fashion. A complete saga of Brutus appeared in Geoffrey of Monmouth's *Historia Regum Britanniae*,[14] which became the pattern religiously copied by writers of history in England. The appeal of the *Historia* was the way Geoffrey related Brutus to the other favorite character of early English history, Arthur. In retelling that popular portion of the *Historia*, writers condensed or embroidered it to suit their purposes. So freely used was this portion that it became known as the *Brut*. The *Historia*, then, rates a special significance because the *Brut* remained throughout the years before the Renaissance "a thriving garden of spurious history in which any transitory nonsense about the remote past might take root and flourish."[15]

The other medieval work which influenced Rastell's efforts, Ralph Higden's *Polychronicon*,[16] was, unlike Geoffrey's *Historia*, literally many chronicles, not just of England but the world. Of course, the English section held the most fascination for the expanding reading public, and significantly, this section demonstrated a trend in historiography which influenced Rastell. Higden, in incorporating Geoffrey's version of British antiquity into the scope of world history, questioned names and dates.[17] Higden's reservations caused some readers to dislike his work, even to reject it, but it became popular nevertheless. Because of its length, the *Polychronicon* was not kept as closely up to date as *Brut*, which added each new king to its long, illustrious line of rulers. The *Polychronicon*, however, had the advantage of placing English history within the scope of world history. Therefore, the two histories offered readers a plethora of experiences and influences from throughout the world and, at the same time, a cause for pride in England as a nation among nations.

Although Rastell refers often to Geoffrey and quotes extensively from the *Polychronicon*,[18] he is most indebted to Robert Fabyan's *Chronycles*.[19] In general, Fabyan reworked Higden and the *Brut*, but his approach seems more literary. He liked to compare differing accounts, but he often refrained from choosing sides. However he questioned the reliability of Geoffrey, Fabyan was content to accept most of the *Brut*, because no other source so attractively accounted for early British history. Since Fabyan's work was not particularly fresh, its fascination for Rastell is difficult to fathom. Yet after publishing *The pastmye* in 1529, the Rastell printers felt a further need for Fabyan; in 1533 William published an edition which, as Reed suggests, may have been intended to make amends for his father's "rather bold and free abbreviation."[20]

Rastell adapted unashamedly from other sources for his own history which, for the work of a legal mind, was disorganized. To bring together the sections on Roman, papal, French, Norman, and British history so randomly placed in Rastell's edition, Dibdin felt obliged to reorganize it. In the original, Rastell uses Christ's birth to divide the book. In the first part, he discusses "kynges of Albanynis," "Romayns," "Brytteyns," and Frenchmen who lived before Christ; of those who lived after the birth of Christ, he treats the "Popis," "emperours of Rome," "Brytteyns or Englishmen," "Frenchmen," "Dukes of Braban and Erlys off Flaunders, and afterward the Normayns" before turning finally to the English rulers through Richard III. Such an arrangement resulted in rambling, disjointed sections, repetitions, and confusion so complete that often Rastell was forced to cross reference his own material.

Despite crude printing and awkward organization, Rastell's history is not without merit. In his use of sources, he demonstrates some degree of critical acumen. If he must be faulted for relying heavily on the *Brut*, *Polychronicon*, and Fabyan's *Cronycles*, he must be credited with recognizing the merit of Fabyan's practice of citing all accounts before choosing the one best calculated to explain a given occurrence. Indeed, for his time Rastell seems careful in citing and evaluating his sources.

In many instances, he refers casually to "other wryters" or prefaces information with the words "some sey" or "some storyes afferme" (11, 25). But frequently, before drawing a conclusion, he cites the source used: "Beda ... Galfryde" (104). He admits his lack of expertise to determine which source has more claim to truth. That for all his usual self-confidence, he recognized the problem of historical veracity is significant. An example of this occurs when, in discussing the story that Frenchmen descended from Hector of Troy, Rastell admits his perplexity: "But as to that opinion I can nother affryme it nor denye: but yet accordyng as the comyn opynyon is moste among them, I shall reherce it as here after shall appere" (7). While hesitant on some points, he does not shy away from criticizing a source, even "ye Britteyn story" of Geoffrey. With relish, he restores information omitted by Geoffrey and even implies that Geoffrey was sometimes wrong.[21]

Rastell's concern for the veracity of sources reveals a scientific objectivity uncharacteristic of his age. In dealing with Stonehenge, he repeats the explanation given by Fabyan (69); this version, borrowed from Geoffrey, states that Merlin took the stones from Ireland. Not content with this explanation, Rastell (105) announces that other men think that Merlin had nothing to do with it; instead, the stones were made "by craft of men, as of sement and morter, made of flynt stonys." To support this theory, he cites two considerations: the hardness of the stones, which suggests they might have been cast, and the impossibility of quarrying and moving stones of such uniform size and color. In scientific fashion, Rastell dismisses the theory of Merlin's involvement, because he is certain that only the natural, technical reasons he presented can explain such a phenomenon.

The other case in which Rastell's scientific interest influenced his scholarship is found in the section concerning the founding of the town of Bath. According to legend, Bladud, a "nigromancyer," made the hot baths through his craft. Rastell rejects this version and prefers the theory that the springs issue naturally from the ground. For the edification of his readers, he explains that natural philosophers believe hot streams cause the hot fumes; he cites Italy with its many warm springs and volcanoes as a cogent example. Then, without pressuring his audience to adopt his point of view, as he had done in the case of Stonehenge, he seems content to let each reader believe what he will (89–90).

The incongruity of Rastell's use of his sources arises from the fact that, while he cites all versions of a particular story, at the same time, he nevertheless accepts at face value some superstitious tales and supernatural events. Particularly in the section on Roman history, he is fond of the phrase "slayn in a tempeste of lightenyng and thouder" to describe the death of notorious tyrants or gifted rulers (11–12). The contemporary, orthodox Christian respect for the Devil helps explain some of this seeming incongruity, for example, Rastell's acceptance of an encounter between Pope Sylvester and the Devil (53).

Perhaps Rastell was being ironic when in the British history section he reports strange happenings in troublesome times: during the reign of William Rufus there occurred earthquakes, two moons, blazing stars, droughts, and "a harde wynter, moreyn of cattell, scarcyte of vyttell, and greate dethe of people"; when King John rules, hailstones as big as hens' eggs were observed, and a strange fish like a man was captured, held for six months, fed raw meat, and thrown back into the sea (175–76); a woman in Edward I's time gave birth to a child with two legs but a double body, while another woman produced a child with a human face but the body of a lion (194). Rastell offers no explanation for these events; he merely recites such occurrences as integral parts of his narrative.

Why he should include such material is puzzling. For all his scientific modernity, Rastell retained belief in the supernatural, not necessarily as the Devil's instrument but as a medium through which the Almighty might warn humanity of impending evil. After all, biblical precedents justified Rastell's acceptance of such superstition. Indeed, for all his effort to find natural causes for phenomena, Rastell is willing to interject moralizing to show that God takes vengeance on evil persons in apt and striking ways.

Admittedly, Rastell's history merits the interest of the modern reader only because it illustrates how an Englishman with humanistic inclinations handled trite material. But when he disagrees or renders value judgments, the study of his history becomes enlightening. An apt illustration is the treatment of printing. Fabyan lauds this invention of a craft "which sen that tyme hath had wonderfull encrease, as experyence at this day provyth" (632). Rastell expounds upon Fabyan's statement: "which is now meruaylously increasyd, whiche hathe ben cause of great lernynge and knowlege, and hathe ben the cause of many thynges and great changes, and is lyke to be the cause of many straunge thyngs here after to come" (269). While retaining the essential facts from Fabyan's comments, Rastell completely rephrases and amplifies it to embrace his own sentiments.

In spite of his respect for Fabyan, Rastell does not hesitate to omit passages from him or to change the other writers' emphases.[22] An omission often indicates Rastell's reluctance to be as critical as Fabyan. Perhaps the humanistic influence gave Rastell the inclination to be more charitable, as illustrated by the sections about Joan of Arc. Whereas Fabyan (642) has harsh words for this girl whose "sorcery and develyshe wayes" were punished by God, Rastell is less outspoken, even though elsewhere he shows no reluctance to cite cases of divine retribution. Rastell does not believe Joan guilty of witchcraft. In fact, he comments favorably upon her role in causing Charles to be crowned king and, in two places, notes how the French called the "mayde of Fraunce," "Le Pusell de dieu" (83, 258–59). Usually so eager to take the English cause against foreigners, such generosity of historical judgment is strange for the patriot Rastell.

Most interesting of all Rastell's adaptations from his sources are his choices and omissions from the body of historical detail concerning the English rulers. Although he used Fabyan or Higden for the material, he exercised, often in a contradictory manner, his own value judgments of rulers. While Fabyan (247) recounts much evil concerning the first William, Rastell (143) is noncommittal. In dealing with Henry II and Edward II, however, Rastell agrees with Fabyan, who blamed the kings themselves for the strife which characterized their reigns (166, 204–5). Whereas Fabyan (438) does not tell how Edward II was slain, Rastell (214) recounts the murder in detail. Similarly, Richard II's death has one version in Fabyan (568) and another in *The pastyme* (241). Also at variance with Fabyan is Rastell's treatment of the Order of the Garter. After repeating Fabyan's account (456–57) of the familiar story of Edward III, Rastell (216–17) gives Richard "Cure de Lyon" the credit for founding the order.

Like Fabyan, Rastell includes sections about Henry V and Agincourt (249) and notes the "obstynacy of the Englysshmen" in renewing the Hundred Years War (259). Regarding the Wars of the Roses, he is less biased than Fabyan or not as pro-Lancastrian. Although Rastell has kind words for Humphrey, duke of Gloucester, and Henry VI, he still maintains a remarkable degree of objectivity for Tudor times, which were so fraught with dynastic loyalties. Concerning the reign of Richard III, with which both narratives end, Rastell makes little effort to deprecate Richard at the expense of Henry VII. It is disappointing that the brother-in-law of More, whose work on Richard caused considerable comment, adds little to the history contemporary to his time. Instead, he follows the lead of Fabyan and merely adds gossipy versions of the murders of the princes.[23]

In the section dealing with English rulers, Rastell occasionally makes original contributions by utilizing, in an interdisciplinary way, knowledge from his other interests. Particularly noteworthy is his concern with heraldry, one of his special hobbies. Because he had employed heraldry in decorating ceilings and building set-designs, he probably judged himself to be an authority on it. His history's woodcuts prominently display the coat of arms of each ruler, a fact suggesting that Rastell himself did these illustrations. He also uses his knowledge of heraldry to disprove the opinion that William Rufus built Westminster Hall. If a hall existed in that ruler's reign, Rastell asserts, it could not be the edifice of his own day, because in its timber and stone are the arms of Richard II, displaying the "flour de lyce" of France, which Rastell declares had not been used by an English king until Edward III (148).

Another antiquarian interest evidenced in *The pastyme* is a concern for establishing the value of money and standards of weights and measures. Rastell's service in 1533 on a commission to test the legitimacy of coinage minted at the Tower verifies his expertise in this area.[24] In his history, Rastell discusses the standards of weights and measures and prices of products during the reigns of Henry III, Edward I, Henry IV (188, 195, 242), in each case comparing them with the standards and values of his day. These digressions also help scholars to date *The pastyme*, for one statement refers to "this present day, whiche is nowe the .xxi. yere of kynge Henry the .viii" (242).

But the strongest interest of Rastell's life, the law, influences his additions to and adaptations of his sources. In fact, *The pastyme* could justifiably be called a legal history of England, if one considers the space given to statutes, ordinances, and assizes. Unlike Fabyan, Rastell uses every opportunity to impress upon the reader the importance for any nation, but particularly England, of rule by a prince who maintains good laws. To stress this point, he extols the actions of those rulers and loyal citizens who sought to further the evolution of good government. Perhaps one reason Rastell wrote his history was the opportunity to place the unique constitutional structure of English government in perspective for public consumption.

Consequently, while Fabyan (320–22) discusses events surrounding the Magna Carta without ever identifying the document, Rastell (178–79) emphasizes its importance and calls it by name. Of course, one must not infer that he considers this document to be a constitution; it was simply a compromise to provide stability, and was subject to renewal. Moreover, he refers casually to the parliament instigated by Simon de Montfort in 1265 as an opportunity to reaffirm and update the Magna Carta (183–90). In this, Rastell condenses Fabyan's account considerably and discusses the event with little emotional involvement. Such is not the case regarding the reign of Edward I. Although Rastell continues to pay little attention to parliament's role, he delights in noting that this king's reign witnessed the creation of "goodly statutes" (193). No mention is made of the Model Parliament of 1295. The historical slant here implies praise for Edward who personally wrought changes in the legal system. This king "ordayned his justyce to make inquisicyons" (198) to determine where crimes had been committed and to collect fines which "fylled his cofers agayne." While hinting at the charge that Edward may have used laws to further his power and economic well-being, Rastell concludes that he did great good within his realm.

Because Rastell related to the passages about law and government, he naturally digressed in these sections. Rastell's *obiter dicta* reveal his real interest in history and perhaps justify the contention that he used *The pastyme* merely to expound his ideas of good government. One example can be found in a section on Roman law and government under Publius Valerius Publicola. This discussion concerns the post of dictator, a position rotated with the stipulation the outgoing official be made answerable for any laws passed during his tenure in office. Rastell implies that this custom explains the success of the Roman reign of justice. At this point (189–90) he digresses to claim that such a system might work well in England if "euery jugge and other offycers havyng auctoryte to execute ye lawis" faced the prospect of being rotated. The knowledge that officials would have to answer to complaints and be subject to punishment for wrongdoing would be healthy for the state of justice in the commonweal. Here Rastell could be commenting about Wolsey who, after remaining in office too long and with too much power, was saved by his death in 1529 from a review of his practices.[25]

Another excursus occurs when Rastell considers the secret elections of the Romans. He admires the opportunity that such a method provided for "trew and indyfferent eleccyons." He comments wistfully on the elections of his own time: "which order, if it were vsyd in this realme, wold cause that there shuld not be so mych troble and malyse, as growith and folowith in our eleccyons, as we se dayly by experyence" (16). Again, Rastell may not have intended this statement as a criticism of individual public officials but merely as a general observation on English government. Ever aware of the didactic possibilities of the media he employed, Rastell here seems unable to refrain from inserting *obiter dicta* designed to remind his readers of the lessons to be learned from history.

Several of Rastell's digressions can be pieced together to provide an image of his ideal ruler. For instance, tyrants who "lak of good ius-tyce" deserve their fate of being deprived "from all kyngly dygnte and honoure."[26] Throughout his history, he praises rulers who stressed books and learning, laws and justice over the pursuit of military vic-tory alone. Of Justinian, he remarks, though he was "greatly gyven to study of bokys, yet he had great vyctory agaynst hys enmys..." (28). Alfred of England won the loyalty of his people "more by iustyce and fayre behestys than by war or cruelty" (126). Edgar of England main-tained "so good iustyce, and dyd so sharp execucyon, that in his days was lytyl felony or robbery vsed" (129). But the most succinct expression of his ideas of good government and the ideal ruler occurs in his postscripts to the abbreviations of Fabyan's account of Edward III: "though that he was occupyed all the tyme of his lyfe in warre, yet he was so cyrcumspecte, that he euer toke hede to the common welthe of his realme, and ordred and stablyssed his lawes meruelously well, and had in his dayes .xxv. or .xxvi. parlyamentes..." (228).

Given such a passage, conjecture is easy. Could Rastell be criticiz-ing Henry VIII or hinting at the course the king should follow? Sig-nificantly lacking is any comparison between Edward III and Henry, though it would have been simple for Rastell to insert words linking the rulers in a matter flattering to Henry. Rastell might have courted royal favor, but he seems oblivious of the opportunity his history affords and seeks only to describe what he, a citizen with legal expe-rience, deems important to good government. In neglecting the smallest chance to curry royal favor, Rastell again proves himself an atypical Tudor citizen.

But in his criticism of sources Rastell reveals a fresh and modern attitude toward problems of historical interpretation. Especially at-tractive have been his comments regarding the early history of Eng-land, in particular the Albion, Brutus, and Arthur legends. To Ferguson Rastell's treatment of these stories is evidence of the existence in early Tudor times of "men whose scholarship or native common sense was at least equal to their patriotism."[27]

This is not to say that no one before Tudor times had questioned the legends of British antiquity. By the fifteenth century, doubts were cast upon the Trojan descent of British royalty by no less a royal personage than Humphrey, duke of Gloucester.[28] Yet by the time of Tudors, such doubts were discouraged; indeed the legends, rather than being rejected, were revived, as the Tudors sought to prove that their reign was the fulfillment of an ancient prophesy that a dynasty would come out of Wales. Even the name of Henry VII's intended heir played upon the connection with times past, and the early Tudor period witnessed a rebirth of chivalric ideals.[29]

At the center of the challenge to the credibility of ancient British history was the Italian humanist scholar Polydore Vergil, whose royally commissioned *Anglica Historia* questioned the popularly accepted stories about the founding of England. Regardless of his respect for the early Tudors, the revival of the Arthurian saga meant little to this transplanted Italian, who approached English history with an objectivity evidenced by few if any before him.[30] Perhaps being foreign-born, he could afford to be skeptical about stories beloved by the English. Yet even Polydore could not entirely cast aside the well-known version of Brutus and Arthur and, therefore, left the matter inconclusive.

To determine Polydore's influence upon Rastell is difficult, because there is no way of knowing if the lawyer-printer read the *Anglica Historia* before its publication in 1534. A case can be made for Rastell's having known Polydore through the More Circle;[31] but, regardless of this connection, Rastell would have known Polydore's reputation and profited from his edition of Gildas' *De Excidio* in 1525, an effort to obtain a correct version of Gildas by collation of two texts. Because Rastell probably used this edition for his references to Gildas,[32] he must have been familiar with the quest for authenticity which characterized Polydore's studies. In spite of the extent Polydore and other historians influenced Rastell, one cannot discount his efforts in compiling his history.

As the critical historian Rastell is seen best in his comments about British antiquity. Yet, this new role clashes with that of Rastell the patriot, for it seems wrong that the champion of the superiority of the English language and English colonization of the New World should assist in debunking the romantic legends of early English heroes. In the beginning of the section about the history of the British Isles,[33] he evidences a reluctance to accept the Albion story of the founding of England without some commonsense reasoning. Here he plays the role of the Renaissance man of reason and scientific intellect who objectively examines legends to decipher truth. After using Fabyan's retelling, Rastell begins his analysis by denying that any one king could have had thirty-two daughters who would marry on the same day. He suggests that this is the stuff of romance, not reality. Likewise, these women could not all have had the same vile dispositions and slain their husbands on the same day. He reasons that at least one of the sisters had to be "somewhat dysposyd to goodnes" and facetiously interjects the aside that "women at this day wyll take my part." Furthermore, that the Devil would have used these women to engender a race of giants is a tale "nother with good feyth nor reason." If such a race began in England, where did it go? Rastell here takes an unsuperstitious stand, in contrast to his statements elsewhere in *The pastyme.*

But this realistic, scientific approach to the Albion legend is best seen in his rejection of the story that thirty-two women set sail from Syria and never touched land until their ship stopped in England, whereupon the land was named after the eldest sister, Albion. The navigator-explorer hastened to argue that such a voyage could not have occurred without a stop for provisions. In addition, he argues that the women's inability to navigate the "many straytis and shawllys" would have prevented such a voyage. If his readers doubt this geographical reasoning, he refers them for an examination of the route to the "quart or Mappa Mundi" found in the "Cosmogrifue."[34]

If this iconoclastic role seems incongruous for the patriotic Rastell, his concluding remarks about this "faynyd fable" clarify any confusion regarding his motives. Explaining that the name Albion probably comes from the Latin for white and refers to the white cliffs at Dover, he announces that his reason for criticizing the legend is the desire to alleviate what he considers an embarrassment for the English. While admitting the appeal of the Albion story, which seems "more meruelouse than tre," he deplores the English belief in it because "other pepull do therefore laugh vs to skorne, and so me semyth they may ryght." Here Rastell the historian is still the patriot. What seemed dubious criticism for a patriot is now revealed to be an effort to raise England's international reputation. Consequently, he remains the humanist seeking through his talents and his press to educate and improve his country. Therefore, as he reasons with his countrymen regarding the Albion legend, his methods are not so much those of a historian as those of a propagandist-patriot who used history to achieve his goals (4).

In dealing with the *Brut*, Rastell treads more cautiously. Perhaps he felt that this story bore more credence and more closely affected the royal house, supposedly tied to Brutus through the genealogical webbing of early British history. For whatever reason, his tone is more moderate, less condescending, and almost noncommittal. Before recounting the story, lifted in abbreviated form from Fabyan,[35] Rastell discusses his sources. To Geoffrey goes the credit for beginning the story Rastell is unable to authenticate through any other source. Somewhat skeptically, he relates how Geoffrey translated into Latin and used as a source for his work an unknown "olde boke written in the britteyn speche." Then he states that Geoffrey omitted both the name of the book and author. The implication here is that Rastell not only thinks Geoffrey less than a scholar but also a fabricator.

Rastell relates how, fearing to accept the *Brut* on the basis of Geoffrey's story, he searched elsewhere. In quest of one source who should have had knowledge of such a person, he turns to Caesar, whose *Commentaries* contain no such story. Obviously if a man of Caesar's integrity never mentioned Brutus, then such a person must be fictitious. To Caesar, Rastell (6) adds Gildas and "holy Beda" as other authorities who do not mention Brutus. As evidence for the rejection of any Brutus story, Rastell notes Bede presented his idea for the founding of his nation, stating the first Britons were from "Lyttyll Brytteyn."

To complete his review of sources, Rastell informs his readers that outside Britain no history can be found which mentions Brutus as its founder. With only Geoffrey's account for proof, Rastell is reluctant to accept the story. After all, he can by returning to his own knowledge of geography propose other more logical methods. He directs the reader's attention to the proximity of Dover to "Gallya." He contends that the appeal of Britain itself—"so fayre so pleasaunt and so fertell"—makes it probable that people from the other side of the channel would have crossed over to fish, to explore, and even to settle. After all, he says, the trip can be sailed in less than three hours (67). Again the practical man of experience settles a scholarly problem, and experience triumphs over learning—a favorite Rastellian theme.

Concluding his examination of the Brutus legend, Rastell acknowledges that, even though the Welshman Geoffrey may have produced a"feyned fable" designed only to bolster his countryman's pride, the story has its attractions. Rastell thus hesitates to cast it aside. Significantly, his refusal to affirm or deny the *Brut*, while perhaps a politic move, is based on reasons relative to his philosophy of history. Not only is the Brutus story fascinating to read, but it also teaches lessons which he deems necessary for public consumption. He therefore offers the *Brut*, notwithstanding all his skepticism, because he believes that from it can be learned the virtues of good governance and, conversely, the misery and devastation visited upon ruler and ruled alike when princes reduce their government to cruelty and tyranny by succumbing to ambition, pride, and sloth. He also finds important the *Brut*'s illustration of the fact that when evil times occur, God intervenes to avenge the victim's wrongs. This divine retribution is an inescapable lesson of history which must be learned by ordinary people and "princis now liuing" (7). History, then, even the "feyned fable" of Brutus, can teach moral wisdom by example.

If Rastell reacted with hostility to the Albion legend and was less than enthusiastic in his acceptance of the *Brut*, his approach to King Arthur is even more original. When first introducing Arthur into the narrative of *The pastyme*, Rastell follows Fabyan's example of questioning sources, like Bede, who should have known about Arthur, but does not mention him.[36] As in his discussions of the Albion and Brutus legends, he questions the authenticity of material, but in this case his approach is that of legal antiquarian. Perhaps he recognized the safety in such an approach or thought it would afford opportunity for novel arguments.

Rastell chose as the crux of his investigation an impression of Arthur's seal of "red wax enclosed in crystal"—with the legend "Patricius Arthurus Britannie Gallie Dacie Imperator"[37]—which hung by the shrine of the Confessor in Westminster Abbey. Rastell challenges its authenticity with three points based upon his knowledge as a legal antiquarian (107). Although the monk at Westminster claimed that Arthur used the seal in conveying a grant to the monastery, Rastell asks how Arthur could have given any gift to a house not founded until after his death. He also doubts any wax could have survived almost a thousand years since Arthur lived. Finally, the legal antiquarian argues that wax seals on documents were not used until the time of William the Conqueror; he further shows that rulers of Arthur's day assigned their hands, not seals, to deeds.

Throughout the passage concerning Arthur's seal, Rastell hid his opinions behind the stylistic device of saying that "some men think it but a thyng faynyd of late by some man hauving effeccion for Arthur." All his contentions begin with the words "they say," a technique which would provide an escape should his remarks offend those in high places. Cautious about declaring himself on the Arthurian debate, he refused to take a definite stand even after attacking what some felt was a chief relic of that hero's existence (107). Thus, although Rastell's antiquarian instincts tell him the Arthurian story is suspect, he believes it harmless.

There is a great jumble of ideas, some new, some old, some original, some borrowed, in *The pastyme.* In general, it repetitiously parrots other histories. High spots, such as the sections on the early English history, are all too rare. And yet their close approach to modern standards of research is impressive given Rastell's unpredictability. By using his logical lawyer's mind he performed, in the analysis of Arthur's seal, a lesser feat analogous to the famous attack by Valla upon the Donation of Constantine. For an early Tudor citizen, not of the first rank of humanists, to exhibit such wisdom and objectivity has impressed scholars to such an extent that one has declared Rastell's precise employment of anachronism to be the first utilization in England of such a technique on a purely historical plane.[38] Kendrick simply called him "wise John Rastell."[39]

If one judges the work by the standards outlined by Ferguson, Rastell does not qualify as an historical thinker. In *The pastyme*, he does exhibit moments when he is "capable of a realistic and systematic examination of evidence, a willingness to stay within the area of what is credible and humanly knowable, and perhaps most significant of all, a recognition of cultures, customs, institutions, of society in short, as a primary objective of historical understanding."[40] Rastell, however, is not writing history for history's sake. His outlook is that of the legal antiquary for whom the most significant theme of his history is the emergence of good laws. Even in attempting to trace this legal theme, he fails to carry his narrative up to early Tudor times or to draw comparisons between his and past society. In some digressions, he makes incidental reference to his own times, but only in those unusual passages about British antiquity does he really confront the differences between his England and the Britain of the past enshrouded in legend. A real sense of perspective, then, is absent from *The pastyme* as a whole.

A new boke of Purgatory

Rastell's entanglement in religious controversy began in 1529 with Simon Fish's *A Supplicacyon for the Beggars.*[41] A diatribe against clerical wealth acquired at the laity's expense, the *Supplicacyon* belongs to the school of religious unrest with Richard Hunne as its special martyr.[42] Fish uses theological arguments to support the socioeconomic basis for his complaints that the average Englishman suffers because a corrupt clergy hide behind doctrines lacking biblical support. One point of contention, though not a major concern for Fish, is the doctrine of purgatory and the practice of paying for clerical prayers to release souls from it. Purgatory is but one example of the injustice of the established church, and Fish employs it and other exaggerated examples in the *Supplicacyon* to incite violent reaction on the part of English laity.

In spite of the "monotonous and commonplace"[43] rhetoric used by Fish, the tract gained such notoriety that More himself felt obligated to answer its charges. In *The Supplicacion of soules*,[44] More obviously enjoyed answering Fish. With his penchant for quips and well-turned phrases, More characterizes Fish's treatise as "flourishing without fruit, subtlety without substance, rhetoric without reason, bold babbling without learning, and wiliness without wit" (12).

More takes as his major topic purgatory, only a minor concern of Fish. Basing arguments upon the scriptural tradition of purgatory's existence, More absolves the clergy and papacy of Fish's charges. To More, denying purgatory was the same as denying St. Peter. Concluding his reply in an emotional fashion, More reminds readers of the cries of loved ones, tormented in purgatory and begging for prayers.[45] The significance of More's reply lies not only on the theological but also the socioeconomic plane. That the chancellor in the Tudor government of 1529 would spend his time and talent replying to Fish's challenge indicates that he sensed some threat of a religiously oriented social revolution.[46]

Why Rastell became ensnared in the Fish controversy cannot be explained, but several reasons may be suggested. Never one to miss an opportunity for advancement, Rastell may have seen his defense of the positions taken by More and Fisher as a way of ingratiating himself with these important men. Since Rastell's relationship with the Mores was strained by this time, perhaps this effort at defending More's position could rejuvenate their friendship. Moreover, Rastell thrived on controversy.

The first two parts of his tract consider questions about God's existence and the soul's immortality. Such subjects give the work the nature of a devotional catechism on issues accepted by most readers. These considerations, ideas against which few sixteenth-century Christians could argue, and a prologue, cast in the vogue of popular travel literature, serve to win the readers' confidence before the controversial subject of purgatory is introduced in the third part. Rastell, a practical man always eager to make money for the support of one of his projects, employs his talents and press to publish a tract on a current religious issue in hopes of appealing to numerous readers.

Never as ardent a Catholic as More, the worldly-wise Rastell utilizes the tract's dialogue-debate form to cast questions on a theological belief about which he and some readers may be less than certain. However, that he sincerely believed in purgatory is not to be discredited completely. Rastell may have envisioned himself as a defender of the faith, even though he had gone to the Continent on behalf of the king's divorce by 1529. In countries other than England, attacks on purgatory went hand-in-hand with espousal of the Reformation. But, in England, Henry, ironically named *Defensor fidei* by the pope for his attack on Luther, entered the Reformation over the issue of divorce, and England's Reformation was basically political, not doctrinal. Thus, in the late 1520s, it was politically astute to be Catholic in theology even while supporting the king and Cromwell on the divorce and the dissolution of monasteries.[47]

More importantly, Rastell's connection with the Hunne case caused his involvement. Doubtless, he saw the challenge of Fish as a weapon to be used by such legal opponents as the Whaplodes, who by 1529 had involved him in several cases concerning the Hunne indenture. By defending the doctrine which, according to Fish, gave the clerics a hold of fear over the people, Rastell could justify the charge of heresy against Hunne and thereby be exonerated for receiving the lands of a heretic. Whatever his reasons, Rastell entered the fray with *A new boke of Purgatory*,[48] the colophon of which mentions that he not only "gedered and compyled" it but also "imprynted and fully fynysshed" it on 30 October 1530.

Although influenced by More's tract, Rastell's work, according to Lewis, "lacks More's humour and dramatic invention and Rastell does not understand his opponents well enough to be dangerous."[49] Following the form of More's attack, he nowhere mentions Fish or his book. Perhaps this failure to aim his work at Fish can be seen as a refusal to dignify Fish with recognition. Rastell might also have assumed most readers already knew his opponent's identity.

Rastell's major concern is to prove the doctrine of purgatory by using "naturall reason and good philosophye," instead of scriptural arguments as More and patristic authorities as Fisher. That Rastell bases his book on More's statements about purgatory adds credence to the suggestion that he undertook this unlikely task to curry favor with his brother-in-law. While More developed some rational arguments to defend purgatory's existence, his major source of proof was scriptural. More maintained that regardless of one's education those who "have learning and perceive not these clear and open texts we marvel of their ignorance" (130). Rastell, perhaps not wishing to seem More's creature, chose a rational approach resulting in a work more concise than More's, but "dry and jejune."[50] Not a theologian, but a lawyer and a man of common sense, Rastell wisely decided to employ "naturall reason and good philosophye." Basing his argument on natural theology, which can be demonstrated by reason without revelation, allows Rastell a different perspective, and this stance had the greater purpose of complementing and supporting the arguments of More and Fisher.

Imitating the *Utopia*, Rastell gives his work the form of a dialogue between a Turk, Gyngemyn, and a German, Comyngo, which allows him to present various viewpoints. These characters are selected to prove the existence of purgatory on a rational basis without the aid of scripture and patristic authority. Rastell's Turk insists that the German use "no maner texte nor authoryte neyther of the olde byble nor of the newe textament" (A3). The creation of these characters (met by the persona Rastell) also allows him freely to advance ideas on the controversial issue of purgatory without taking sides himself or asking his readers to do so, and without fear of being reprimanded by the authorities for presenting particular arguments. The device of a Turk (non-Christian) who demonstrates from reason the truth of the doctrine of purgatory in opposition to a misguided German Protestant who has supposedly seen the light of revelation is ironic and another indication of the *Utopia*'s influence. In the prologue, Rastell sets the scene by describing how, when he traveled "into dyuers farre countreys in the eest partys," he came to a large city. There he met two gentlemen, "well lernyd bothe in morall phylosophye and naturall." The three spent hours discussing current events, such as the progress of the Turks throughout Europe, and Rastell includes historical data to add an authentic flavor.

The prologue sets forth seven rational arguments against the doctrine of purgatory. As if already sympathetic to the cause to which he was to be converted, Rastell states the objections to purgatory almost more enthusiastically than the arguments which disprove them. Basically his seven points can be condensed into three contentions. First, because God is merciful and just, His forgiveness for sins requires no further punishment than repentance. Purgatory serves no purpose, because man need not suffer if God has forgiven him. Second, because man's immortal soul must have infinite joy or pain immediately after death, the idea of a place between mortal-immortal existence is nonsense. Since death separates the finite body from the immortal soul, the spirit cannot know the finite pain of purgatory. Third, man need not concern himself with a ritual of purification designed to make all men equal, because heaven has various levels. A less pure soul can know infinite joy at a lower level than a saint.

The first two parts of *A new boke of Purgatory* deal with the "merveylous exystens of God" and "the immortalyte of mannys soul." Only in the third part does the dialogue concern purgatory. These first two parts are repetitious and full of verbose and ineffectul passages. Of interest, however, are several themes recurrent in Rastell's works. Revealing his antitheological bias and foreshadowing his conversion, he reiterates his thesis concerning purgatory. "For there is nothynge in the worlde shall alter and chaunge a mannes mynde and beleue so well and surely / as shall the judgemet of his owne reason" (B4ᵛ).

In several revealing passages discussing the everlasting nature of the divinity, Rastell considers the frailty of man's moment of earthly life. Man knows pleasures "durynge one lytell moment whyche is shorte" (B3), but God in His eternal existence has such wisdom He comprehends the whole of man's life. God contains no "mutabylyte / and change & augmentacyon of knowlege" (B3). Rastell writes forcefully about such undisputable topics. But, when treading into debatable subjects, like purgatory, he is less convincing as a writer-propagandist, perhaps because he himself is undecided upon such issues.

Accompanying the belief about God is another Rastellian theme: the qualities of nobility that make man God's most excellent earthly creation. Rastell lists three definitions of nobility, explored in depth in *Gentylnes*: "noblenes is that whyche hath leste nede of foreyne help" (A4ᵛ); "understanding is the cause of the moost noble and moost worthy beyng" (A5ᵛ); and, man is the most "worthy and noble of all his creatures in yerth because he is moste lyke unto God" (B1). In combining these definitions, Rastell belabors the point about man's place in the hierarchy of creatures, where man and beasts have, unlike trees and rocks, "a quycknes of a lyfe . . ." (A5ᵛ), but man alone has understanding. Rastell confidently concludes that man's understanding gives him the qualities to reason through a problem and find the truth.

As if unaware of the contradictions, the propagandist proceeds in the second part to bemoan man's lot as a noble creature. While admitting that only man knows how to honor God, it seems unfair that man's life "is more wreched sorowfull and worse / than the lyfe of any other brute beste here in yerthe" (C2). While beasts have natural coverings for their bodies, men suffer from naked bodies which need protection. In an almost melancholy mood, Rastell remembers the life of beasts is not man's lot: man has a rational nature.

Attempting to interject a more positive tone, Rastell evaluates the advantages of the mind, but he continually returns to the disadvantages of rational thought which cause men to suffer. Inherent in this discussion is the story of the fall. Since man lost Eden, he must endure "mych veracyō / thought / study & unquietnes of mynde / whyche the brute bestes indure not / for though that man knoweth surely that he shall dye & oft taketh thought therefore / yet the brute bestys have no knowlege of theyr deth / nor take no thought therfore" (C2ᵛ). These ideas, not present in his other writings, denote a nostalgia for earlier days. Reflecting upon the ill effects of man's progress in becoming a noble, rational creature, the nostalgia and pessimism of this passage perhaps indicate that age and the difficulties of life were beginning to subdue Rastell.

In an effort to explain unhappiness, Rastell discusses covetousness. The desire for riches and honor or the fear of their loss contributes to man's miserable lot. In a passage remarkably revelatory of his life, he speaks of the "great payne laboure and study / veracyon and unquyetness of mynde for the obteynyng of such thynges" (C2ᵛ). If the happiness for having material possessions comes from God, then Rastell reluctantly concedes that man must accept it as part of eternal wisdom. From this discussion of miseries Rastell argues that God in His wisdom must have ordained immortality for the soul as compensation for man's struggle to obtain worldly riches and honor.

Rastell then moves to the soul's immortality, a belief necessary for any discussion of purgatory. It can be proved by reason if one accepts God's eternal nature and continuity within the world's mutability. To amplify this explanation, Rastell, relying on his favorite subject, postulates that, because everything in the world is composed of the "iiij elements," everything in the world merely changes forms: "mater euer remayneth" (D2^v). The body decays to dust; the soul meets another fate (D3).[51]

Rastell next announces that man's soul makes him unique. Throughout *A new boke of Purgatory*, Rastell uses soul, understanding, and reason interchangeably. Undisturbed by such confusion of terms, he proceeds to explain the soul, which he believes exists fully developed before birth. Life becomes a process of discovering what is in the soul (D4–D4^v). Man does not himself acquire knowledge but rather the methods to reveal that knowledge already placed within him. To illustrate these ideas, Rastell's Turk uses the analogy of the harper and his harp; there can be no music until the harp is strung and in tune; only then can the harper play (D3^v).[52] Similarly, man must use his mind to unlock the knowledge contained in his soul before he can be fully rational.

Realizing a problem arises from such ideas, Rastell explains what differentiates one man from others: if all souls are alike, why do men differ? He explains that the body hinders the soul and enslaves it in a cage of skin and bones. The perfectibility of a man's soul depends on how damaged it is by that individual's bodily appetites or "humours" (E1^v). Excessive eating and drinking dull the mind and cause varying reactions. Some men possess different "humours" for learning of "musyke as dyscant and syngynge," while others learn "scyens of logyke or phylosophy" (E1^v–E2). Some can learn both; others are too dull to learn either. As a warning to all, Rastell recalls insanity is the sign of a totally depraved mind, whose soul has no hope of salvation. When the brain is damaged, understanding is impaired, and the soul is made inactive (E1–E1^v).

The eternal wisdom of the souls of all men is further explained in a discussion of dreams. Rastell believes that dreams are significant avenues of communication between human and divine beings. The body in motion distracts the soul, so man can only think in repose. Consequently, only after death can the soul be free from the body (E2^v). During life the best approximation of this freedom occurs during dreams when the soul, removed from physical limitations, can move beyond earthly bounds. Man can foretell death or bodily harm in his dreams, and Rastell, as some of his contemporaries, believes dreams are sacred and not to be ignored (C3–C4).

After such a lengthy proof of the soul's immortality, Gyngemyn concludes that men who deny such reason do so to justify their evil ways. The implication is that all readers who deny purgatory also deny the soul's immortality and are therefore evil (B4). Spoken by the Turk, a nonbeliever but a rational man, this passage is meant to condemn those Christians who refuse even rationally to accept the doctrine of purgatory. Actually, this argument worked against Rastell, because his opponents were quick to note some of his proofs for the soul's immortality were not without fallacy. Rastell, perhaps realizing this failure, concludes his argument with the contention that even if there were no immortality, men should live as if there were: the virtuous life "by no possbylyte can neuer hurt the" (C1ᵛ). Living according to such principles allows one to prosper as the Marchaunt in *Gentylnes* observes. But fear is still the better reason for belief in the soul and purgatory.

In the last sections, Rastell confronts, in a superficial way, several conventional objections to purgatory. Such arguments, although not intellectually contemptible, fail to do him credit. Perhaps the dialogue resulted from hasty, unconcentrated thought and should not be judged by the same standards as the rest of his writings. Whatever the reasons, *A new boke of Purgatory* stands significantly as an indication of the confusion and controversy surrounding a period of crisis in Rastell's life when he was forced to reevaluate his political, intellectual, familial, and religious positions.[53]

Rastell presents as a major reason for belief in purgatory the standard argument of fear. Against this reason, Comyngo raises the objection that repentance, even a deathbed confession, is all that God requires. The Turk weakly objects by claiming that such a line of argument presumes to compel God to obey rules. Besides, men cannot be sure that God will be satisfied with mere repentance (F1). The Turk's argument figures importantly in the last section. Rastell uses it to confound all his opponents without feeling constrained by it himself.

When Comyngo objects to purgatory by insisting that man's infinite soul must have eternal joy or pain, not finite purgatory, Rastell's Turk counters by decreeing that sins have degrees. The Turk advances the orthodox doctrine of the necessity of satisfaction for all sins committed. By way of proof, Rastell describes a prince who, after a person is found guilty and repents, can still kill or pardon him. If a prince acts thus, God in whose image man is made can also demand full restitution (F1ᵛ–F3). Here Rastell assumes that God acts like man and that human justice is a reflection of divine justice.

Parallels between divine justice and earthly legal institutions develop this part of the natural theology argument for the atonement of sins, and perhaps such arguments reveal some of Rastell's philosophy of law.

As if realizing the weakness of his arguments, Rastell turns to another objection to purgatory. The German insists that souls less pure than others can still serve God and illustrates this point by describing a man who, after an unsuccessful attempt to clean soiled linen, uses it not at the high table but for menial chores. To confute this argument, the Turk proposes that heaven has no degrees, since any impurity of souls there would be anathema. Moving to the next question of where purgatory is located, Rastell reminds his readers of the folly of such a query; God could find a place for purgatory though man cannot.

After this cursory discussion of the topic proposed in the title, Rastell returns to the fundamental issue of God's justice and again exhibits the fallacy of attributing human traits to God by assuming that human justice reflects divine justice. This, however, may reveal Rastell's conception of law and his belief that the best human justice mirrors divine inspiration. He believes in a harsh Old Testament conception of justice. God's mercy does exist but not without divine retribution. God does forgive, but His justice requires punishment. Rastell will tolerate no other explanation of divine justice. He describes a vengeful God, mindful of human frailties but relentless in meting out punishments. Even if God does forgive, man's inhumanity to his fellowman cannot be as easily forgiven.

Concluding his dialogue, Rastell, through the rational arguments of the Turk, causes the German to reaffirm his faith in purgatory as a place for the purification of unforgiven sins, as a last chance for sinners to repent, as a reminder of the wages of sin, and ultimately as a means through "drede of god" (H4) of bringing all men to divine wisdom. The last point reveals a characteristic twist to Rastell's arguments. Realizing man's infinite capacity for evil, the lawyer-propagandist envisions religion as a "brydel of law" (H4) to curb emotions. Man does good not so much through the love as the "drede of God." A negative approach to religion, it nevertheless restrains man from the conditions inevitably accompanying the rejection of belief in purgatory (H4).

Rastell must have been disheartened, because his contribution to the purgatory controversy received little notice until John Frith wrote his *A disputacion of purgatorye*.[54] Frith, a Cambridge reformer influenced by Tyndale, returned to England in July 1532 from exile in Flanders. He had already entered the debate over purgatory when he published *A disputacion* on the Continent in 1531. Back in England Frith hastened to reprint it in London in 1533.[55] The work, though not as significant as Tyndale's, nevertheless offered a lively, intelligent answer to the three defenders of purgatory.

Frith does not take seriously Rastell's highly orthodox arguments for purgatory's existence; and, like a radical reformer in revolt against the scholastic tradition of natural theology, he dismisses rational arguments as meaningless, since religious truths must be revealed. In fact, Rastell's use of "naturall reason and good philosophye" and his rejection of revelation cause his characters to do much falacious reasoning, because many theological questions are beyond the bounds of reason. Frith riddles Rastell's "natural philosophy" with damaging shrapnel coming from one major blast—Rastell's avoidance of revelation makes him a non-Christian who cannot talk of purgatory or heaven. Frith reports he was "mervellously desirous and tickled" (87) to see the seven objections to purgatory Rastell thought popular among wayward Catholics. These reasons, Frith contends, are "not worth one bean" (87). Because his book is based on natural reason, Rastell has denied the scriptures "unto which our reason must ever be obedient" and been "extremely injurious unto Christ and His precious blood" (88). Frith argues that purgatory does indeed exist in two forms: the word of God and more importantly the cross of Christ, not the material one, but the spiritual one "which is adversity, tribulation, worldly depression" (90–91). Beyond these two purifying agents, no other purgatory exists.

Although Frith devastates Rastell's arguments, his attitude toward him is contradictory, and he seems genuinely concerned to convert him. Recognizing the motivations for Rastell's book and the qualifications of the writer, Frith gives a character sketch cruel in its truth: "Rastell ... which is a Printer, ... and of Master More's Alliance, which also coveteth to counterfeit his kinsman, although the beams of his brains be nothing so radiant nor his conveyance so commendable in the eyes of the wise" (94). Then charitably, Frith declares he hopes Rastell "might perceive his own ignorance, and return again into the right way" (95). The same sentiment applies to any deceived through his book, "and I trust there are but few, except they be very ignorant" (95).

Frith's book reaped its desired, but unexpected, harvest: Rastell's conversion! John Foxe said, in praise of Frith's accomplishment: "But he, as a Hercules fighting not against two only, but even with them all three at once, did so overthrow and confound them, that he converted Rastell to his part."[56] Actually, the events were more complicated. Rastell was never an ardent Catholic. Even in his Coventry days, he was considered unorthodox. By 1529 he had shown indications of moving away from the strict position of More. Moreover, by 1533 he had come within the sphere of Cromwell and Cranmer as one of the humanist-citizens called to service to offset the More defection. Not as capable of giving clear-cut answers to controversial questions as other literary forms, the dialogue-debate projects an indecisive position. Its arguments against purgatory's existence are sometimes stronger than those claiming it exists. Avoiding the controversial subject until the third part, Rastell defers the heart of the matter as long as possible. All these points betray its ineffectiveness as powerful controversial literature and seem to reveal conflicting beliefs which render Rastell less than capable of dealing decisively with the issue.

Obviously, the Frith report disturbed Rastell, for he replied in 1533. More and Fisher paid no heed to Frith's attacks, but Rastell wrote a second book on purgatory which came into Frith's hands. No copy of Rastell's book exists. On one of the sheets of the Court of Requests case, "Rastell versus Walton," Reed discovered what appears to be a scrapped beginning of the rejoiner.[57] Frith's answer to Rastell's retort does, however, exist. In 1533, while imprisoned in the Tower, Frith wrote *An other boke against Rastell named the subsidye or bulwarke to his first boke / made by John Frith prisoner in the Tower*, and its prologue gives some facts about the conversion. Touched by the wit which Frith exhibited under difficult circumstances in prison, Rastell was affected as much by the conditions of the writing as by the persuasive rhetoric. Being in some ways more worldly-wise than More, perhaps Rastell saw the inevitable religious change. For such a rational materialist as Rastell seems to be, it is better to adapt to changing times and live than to resist and die. Again, in another way, Rastell is not his brother-in-law.

Indecisive considerations motivated Rastell's foray into religious battle, and throughout *A new boke of Purgatory* shows the lawyer-humanist's inability to deal with theological matters. Perhaps of all his activities, he failed most miserably as a religious controversialist, and yet one must credit the grace with which he faced his defeat. A good loser, Rastell with typical enthusiasm endorsed his opponent's position. Intemperate as ever, he became as erratic a Protestant as he had been a Catholic. If he was a martyr by virtue of his death in the Tower, the cause was not so much his Protestant beliefs as his uncontrollable spirit which led him to plunge precipitately into whatever cause he chose to champion.

In attempting to focus upon those sections in Rastell's prose work which best illuminate the early Tudor period, one must realize that these writings reflect the thoughts of an individual who was influenced by others. These influences were distilled into what seemed a suitably workable system of thought for Rastell, an eclectic thinker who had a penchant for assimilating the ideas of others and applying them. Thus, when examining the prose works for evidence of creative thinking, one must remember that Rastell remained a man of reason who based his arguments on practical considerations derived from his legal training.

Significantly, Rastell brings to his writing of history and religious propaganda the attitude of a practical man trained for the legal world, but very much part of the complexity and confusion of Tudor society. Thus, when he wants to, he can view his material with the same objectivity with which he studies common law cases or plans for his next printing venture. The difficulty in his prose works, so unorganized and inconsistent, arises probably from his multiplicity of activities. He more than likely wrote during snatches of free time between his legal, parliamentary, governmental, printing, and familial duties. As a consequence, the prose works lacked concentrated attention and suffer thereby; nevertheless, they remain as testaments to the earnestness of Rastell's lifelong pursuit to be an active member of the Tudor commonweal.

Chapter Four
The Practical,
Patriotic Humanist

Variously lawyer, judge, stage builder, chief of army transport, trench engineer, printer, architect, colonizer, political and religious rebel, historian, playwright, designer of pageants, member of Parliament, and pamphleteer, Rastell and his vitality are appealing. In his versatility, he is very much a Renaissance man. And, in his own ways, as an active citizen from the best of the English middle class, he is, ironically, a better example than his kinsman, More, of the practical, patriotic Tudor humanist. Throughout his activities, Rastell had a single goal—to serve the English commonweal. Though self-appointed, this sense of duty was sincere, and while his methods sometimes appear overly zealous, the earnestness of his motives is above reproach.

The catalytic event in Rastell's life was his association with More, which exposed him to the humanists and launched him on his quest for acceptance by his kinsman and his humanist acquaintances. In the process, Rastell sought success in many humanistically oriented professions. Of average intellect and middle class, he would not have qualified for the new nobility of action and mental attainment or for the old nobility whose hereditary claim he disputed. Although he dabbled in many professions, he attained preeminence in none. His consuming interest in law brought him neither a distinguished career on the bench nor renown as a legal theorist. His many projects ended mostly in failure and seldom garnered even a modicum of enthusiasm from the public he labored to serve.

Yet it is difficult not to admire Rastell, even to see in him traces of greatness; he was potentially exceptionally gifted. Many of his failures can be blamed on his troubled times. Rastell was perhaps too confined in a society marred by conflict, suspicion, and intolerance. In the freer age of the later Renaissance, he might have fared better, for men of his versatility flourished under Elizabeth I. In his times, his efforts seldom met with encouragement, yet he moved on from each disappointment to other projects, intent always on personal success and service to the commonwealth—goals of a practical, patriotic humanist.

Of his many professions, that of printer best illustrates this humanist influence distilled by his own concepts of patriotic service. His aim to educate the common people through the use of English suggests that he was a popularizer. But, as a popularizer, his goals were not merely to attain financial success or adulation from common people. He was sincerely attempting to simplify complex concepts and make the ideas of the humanists accessible to others. For these reasons, Rastell printed plays and other literary works, jest books, legal treatises, a history, and religious and controversial tracts with little regard to whether public tastes corresponded to his.

Rastell's Use of Drama

The drama as a stage upon which to present his ideas was of particular interest to Rastell. Because of his use of this medium to propagandize his causes, he fits the epithet given him by Frederick Boas, "an early Tudor Bernard Shaw."[1] How many plays Rastell wrote and printed is not important; the ideas he believed worthy for public consumption in them is important. Few of these ideas are new; the novel feature is their presentation. Two themes recur: patriotism and the worth of the English language. Indeed, Rastell has been called "the earliest outspoken champion of the vernacular."[2]

Throughout *The Four Elementis* there appears a strain of national pride. In setting forth justifications for colonization, Rastell begins with the reason Englishmen should be first to take possession of the new lands, undertake building and habitation, and reap a "memory perpetuall" (767). Such enterprise will bring honor both to the realm and the king. Honor and glory are worthy reasons for exploration, but Rastell, the practical humanist, adds the humanitarian touch and reminds his audience of the unsaved souls in the New World (768–86). Rastell's reason for colonization also combines national pride with concern over commerce. He projects the wealth that might be derived from the raw materials of the New World, in particular, wood and fish (799–810). He envisions England developing trade with the New World as an alternative to depending upon foreign merchants. Controversy over fishing rights had brought wars with the French, and a strong commercial relationship with the New World

would free England from these international involvements and
strengthen her prestige.

Another recurrent concern of Rastell's found in this interlude is
his emphasis upon promoting literature in English. He laments the
lack of good books in the vernacular and argues that English is as
pliable as Greek, Latin, or any "moder tonge" (23). The trouble is
that so few clerks take the pains to translate (24–28). His concern
is not for educated Englishmen who read several languages, but for ignorant or semi-educated Englishmen (29–35). Rastell has no kind
words for those who have the ability to translate worthwhile works
but compile love stories or print ballads instead. In his opinion, such
waste of talent and public time is unforgiveable (36–42). He announces in his prologue to the interlude that he will not pursue such
a course of idleness, flattery, and conceit. Lamenting the ignorance of
his countrymen, he attributes it to the lack of learned works in the
English language and announces his intention to fill this void (43–
49).

Rastell's Use of Chaucer

And so Rastell did, by printing an edition of Chaucer's *The parlyment of fowles* which proves interesting, particularly because of its
five-verse introduction attributed to him. In this paean to the author,
Chaucer's works are compared to Aurora whose heralding of light dis-
pels the blackness of night. Rastell implies an understanding of the
transitional nature of Chaucer's works, though he may not have meant
that the dark should be interpreted as the Middle Ages. Yet with his
reverence for verse, he, as other Renaissance writers, cannot but realize the debt Englishmen owed to Chaucer for their style.

Rastell as Humanist Lawyer-Printer

But Rastell's legal works, forming the core of his printing, bear the
strongest witness to the beliefs governing his activities as printer,
lawyer, and articulate citizen. Despite his many avocations, Rastell was
by profession a lawyer and brought to printing his incurable interest
in the intricacies of the law. Thus, he could justify publishing year
books, abridgments of statutes, and a law dictionary. But more idealistic motivation came from the influence of the More Circle.[3] Of all
the tenets of humanism, the More Circle's emphasis upon the importance of common law and education appealed most to Rastell,

whose basic social and intellectual principles were always closely related to his grounding in the English common law as an instrument for the betterment of the citizenry.

There had to be dedication of purpose on the part of any printer who dared undertake, with no certainty of profit, the production of law books.[4] Printers were reluctant to undertake these law books because they demanded expert handling. However rewarding producing law books may have been, his sales would have been small, even with the general patronage of the legal profession. Rastell could pride himself on producing books of good quality; in this he was motivated less by profit than by a satisfaction derived from making available to his peers invaluable guides in their profession, which he believed necessary for maintenance of the common good.

This is not to deny Rastell's interest in realizing a profit from the publication of law books. Never above combining humanist idealism with practical realism, Rastell decided to expand his potential public by translating from French and Latin into English those laws he felt important for the average Englishman to understand. General social betterment was never far detached from his personal betterment. Yet he performed his duties as law printer zealously, because he was far from being completely selfish in motivation. He did believe in the knowledge of laws as a means of individual enrichment. The enthusiasm he exhibited for the tedious tasks of compiling, translating, and printing law books denotes his high-minded purposes. Indeed, never was he more involved in all stages of printing than when producing his law books. While critics have noted the mediocrity of the style of the prefaces to these works,[5] his attempt, nevertheless, ranks as the first in the Tudor era to address itself to the average citizen and educate him in the law which had made the English way of life peculiarly blessed.

For Rastell, the common law remained the chief source of England's greatness, and through his peers he had the means to bring compilations of it within reach of a public beginning to emerge as a source for book sales. Rastell was not influenced by the trend to accent Roman law as the basis of the English system, except in the negative way in which the entire More Circle reacted to it. Patriotic in response to any suggestion of receiving the Continental system, the More Circle believed the common law,[6] grown from ancient Germanic custom, developed by legislation from throne, parliament, and decisions of judges, was the only answer to the past and present needs of the English people. Therefore, any program of reform through education espoused by the More Circle included no change in English law except to make its importance clear for the average citizen by expressing it in language comprehensible to an untrained public.

Inherent in all Rastell did was a faith in the perfectibility of man, not as sophisticated as that espoused by More and Erasmus, but nevertheless a belief that man can learn and that from the knowledge of the truth can come justice and virtue. The real purpose of law was to assure justice and peace, and laws should be stated as clearly and succinctly as possible so that men can receive these blessings. Laws held the commonweal together, but both ruler and subject must understand and consent to abide by the laws to achieve goodness. Positive law expressed the will of God, which Rastell and others saw as happiness for all men.[7] Thus, all that was needed to bring God's will to fruition in human life was education of the individual in those laws evolved by the legal profession under royal control.

Rastell's Law Printing

Rastell's law printing can be divided into two types: those printed by the lawyer for lawyers, and those designed for the general public. Rastell had several types of legal writings from which to choose.[8] Large folio editions of statutes at large might be printed, or, as was done more often, smaller editions of statutes promulgated year by year since the last large collected edition. More popular with printer and public were the abridgments of statutes, and especially the year books. The records of medieval common law cases could be printed completely, separately, or as abridgments of these annual reports. Early printers recognized the uniqueness of year books as a guide to the past and a record of past precedents. Rastell saw a market among his fellow lawyers for these legal notebooks: perhaps even the general public would like the words, actions, and idiosyncracies of the courtroom. Furthermore, because the year books were a peculiarly English product, a printer-patriot could take pride in their production, particularly as he believed all people, not just lawyers, should understand the intricacies of common law.[9]

Rastell apparently published three year books, possibly more. While he recognized the worth of year books as the basis for legal printing, Rastell shifted early in his printing career to publishing abridgments as a more effective means of reaching the public. As a result, in 1513, he published *Liber Assisarum*, a concise version of the legal year book of the reign of Edward III. Except in its prologue, Law French is used, because the work was designed for lawyers. And yet its prologue, in which Rastell attempts to explain his philosophy of law and to justify his printing, presumably was directed to the general public, because it is in English. This prologue makes the book invaluable to the historian of Tudor intellectual history, for it lifts its content from the albeit interesting level of early legal printing to the plateau of information concerning what early Tudor citizens thought about themselves, their government, and their world.

Of the four prologues Rastell wrote for his legal publications, that to the *Liber Assisarum*[10] not only is the longest but also the most rambling and redundant. In his title, Rastell states his theme: "in praise of Law: that the commonweal does not consist in riches, power, not honours, but in good laws." The message seems aimed at the reader uneducated in the law and more subtly at a prince who may have forgotten its importance. Rastell presents his case in the tone of one assured of the truth and wisdom of his words: of course, everyone knows "the thing that is ever among men most had in reputation and esteemed most digne and most universally desired is the public and commonweal of their country." The man who endeavors to serve the commonweal will be "most magnified and lauded, best loved, and most honorable [and] renowned." Obviously styling himself as such, Rastell invites his readers to join him in discovering the best way to understand the commonweal.

Admitting the difficulty experienced by learned men who sought to define the commonweal, Rastell proposes to simplify the problem. His readers have been confused in the past because those men defined "commonweal" variously as an abundance of riches, power and strength, honor and glory, or as all three intermixed. Rastell does not pause to discuss these definitions at length but manages to point out the selfish motivations underlying each of them.

There then follows a section of Rastellian logic. To prepare the way for his own definitions, he proposes to consider the problem in terms of good and evil. After all, common*weal* means common good not common *evil*.[11] If any definition deserves the epithets of esteem, Rastell maintains that definition must be good because God, "the foundement of all goodness," has given to every man "a common and an universal love and zeal" to recognize goodness as the essence of a *commonweal*. No Machiavellian ethics influence this preface. Evil methods produce evil results. No commonweal can exist if produced by riches, power, and glory at the expense of poverty, feebleness, and shame. Another definition must be found.

The commonweal, Rastell is saying, is the common good of all, not just a few. Therefore, if any person suffers ill, all suffer. Having reached midpoint in his preface, Rastell favors the reader with the true definition: "Which now under correction, after mine opinion, the commonweal resteth neither in increasing of riches, power, nor honour, but in the increasing of good manners and conditions of men whereby they may be reduced to know God, to honour God, to love God, and to live in a continual love and tranquility with their neighbours. For the which thing to be attained, it is to men most expedient to have ordinances and laws...."[12] Here, then, is the crux of Rastell's political philosophy, the panacea to all ills. Man is like a horse; he needs the bridle and spurs of the law to guide and restrain him. Rastell notes that nature has not designed mankind instinctively to use "good manners and conditions." Man is not basically good, but neither is he bad, only sidetracked until education can lead him to the path of goodness.

At the basis of Rastell's philosophy is the belief in the educability of his fellowmen. Man can change his position, improve his environment, and bring about the commonweal. Rastell proposes the creation of a community of persons who, regardless of rank and background, by good manners and good conditions, can care for their fellowmen. There is no suggestion of commonly shared wealth, power, or glory. Nor is democracy discussed. What Rastell seems concerned about is that all men live peaceably and willingly under the laws promoting commonweal. He defines this ideal existence: "to use good manners and conditions, and thereby to honour, to dread, and to love God, and virtuously to live among their neighbours in continual peace, and tranquility, in firm concord and agreement, in a unity of will and mind, and in sincere and pure love and charity...."[13] Actually Rastell has combined the Golden Rule, great commandment of Jesus, and thirteenth chapter of Corinthians, and yet he sounds strangely unclerical, as if he were only paying lip service to a convention to gain reader support. To remove the phrase about God would not seriously alter the formula. Thus, if the wording of this remedy for the ills of the commonweal sounds more legally than theologically moralistic, it merely serves to illustrate that Rastell was more a legal than a Christian humanist.

There is a section in the preface to *Liber Assisarum* explaining that, if the providence of God leads nature to produce food, shelter, and clothing for man, certainly this same providence will guide man more diligently in creating laws "most necessary and to the augmenting of the divine honour." Logically Rastell concludes that if God helps make laws and all from God is goodness, then the laws, themselves, must be good. And because Rastell has already shown the commonweal can only prosper by a good method, law must provide the answer. The purpose of the entire preface appears here; Rastell wants to convince his readers that law and the legal profession have made and continue to make the greatest contributions to the commonweal.

Rastell's next publication concerning law was Fitzherbert's *La Graunde Abbregement de le Ley.* This work has neither an introduction nor a complete table of cases discussed, but in 1517, a year after the publication of Fitzherbert's book, Rastell filled the void by publishing a table with a Latin prologue.[14] The major interest of this work is not the time or effort expended in compiling it, but the prologue in which Rastell airs more humanistic ideas about law, the commonweal, and his relationship to both. In its prologue, the printer sets forth his definitions of and theories about the three kinds of universal laws. Unfortunately for students of Rastell these definitions are too brief and rudimentary. Perhaps Rastell felt unqualified to theorize. Or his summary treatment here may have been influenced by the belief that, because his table referred to Fitzherbert's *La Graunde Abbregement*, a publication used mostly by lawyers, his reading audience would be drawn mainly from the legal profession. This consideration, which prompted the ardent proponent of the vernacular as an educative implement to use Latin, probably also led Rastell to sense the superfluousness of expounding at length what would be common knowledge to lawyers.

In its thirty-four lines, Rastell expresses more sincerely than in any other place his belief in Divine Providence. His initial premise is that God has created a diversity of beings to share in His goodness. Governing His diverse creation are three universal laws: divine, human, natural. Rastell gives orthodox definitions to these laws with little explication. Perhaps knowing his ideas not to be particularly innovative, he merely affirms the standard definitions. And yet the simplicity of his preface, a simplicity absent from other prologues, reveals the respect with which Rastell viewed his profession.

Apparent too in Rastell's brief prologue is a characteristic theme of that transitional time in early Tudor England: the emphasis on the right of the individual to develop his intellect and live freely in a society governed by laws. This is commonly held by the humanists, but Rastell moves beyond the individual to mankind, who alone of God's creations possesses the ability to obey all three facets of universal law. The way of righteousness is plain to Rastell's pragmatic mind. The order of the universe exists; to disrupt it is death. Evident here is the Tudor passion for stability and coherence, manifested politically, intellectually, in virtually every realm of endeavor.[15] Rastell does not say, but clearly believes, that if man is denied the right to own property, settle his own affairs, and enjoy personal freedom, then anarchy will exist. Furthermore, tyranny results from disobedience to the laws of God, particularly human law. Made by man with man's greatest gift—reason—human law preserves tranquillity, the desired end of good government. Rastell does not develop this theory; indeed, he does little more than recite definitions.

Beyond these definitions, Rastell's only statement is the affirmation that the three laws do not contradict each other. The complete man will rise above natural law, obey human law, and revere divine law to escape death by living in tranquillity on earth until he reaps heavenly reward. Rastell implies that the man who follows this formula will be the perfect citizen, and, together with like-minded citizens, will fashion the commonweal. Rastell proposes that just as a person is obligated to fight for his country, so he naturally should be willing to conserve the laws of his land. This plea to patriotism relieves the otherwise dull legal preface. It is obvious that in Rastell's eyes, his self-assigned legal duties are as important to the nation's well-being as the responsibilities of a military leader. What good would there be in saving the country from invasion unless the country were a commonweal? And what characterizes the commonweal? He who preserves the laws. Turning in its accustomed grooves, Rastellian logic completes another cycle.

Evidently elated with the success of Fitzherbert's book, Rastell undertook his own abridgment. In October 1519, *The Abbreviation of Statutes*, the first book of abridgments presented entirely in English, appeared from his press. Rastell functioned as his own translator and provided readers with a prohemium. Confusion surrounds the original edition, but numerous reprints of it exist and all include the same prohemium.[16] The success of the series of law abridgments indicates at least an increasing awareness of the right of the English public to know about, perhaps even participate in, the workings of the commonweal. And for this awakening of the people's interest in their government, environment, and heritage of laws, the lion's share of credit must be given to men like Rastell.

Aware of his work's novelty, Rastell wrote a preface sometimes called "naive and intimate."[17] Granted, it does not match the intellectual level of his other prefaces, but this time Rastell was writing for those ignorant of legal history. If he seems condescending toward his audience, perhaps he may be forgiven because of his sincerity of purpose. Whereas formerly he had been a lawyer writing mainly for lawyers and those outside the profession interested and educated enough to digest the specialized law books he offered, in this edition of the *Abridgments* his intended audience is the general public. Therefore, he simplifies and overstates for the sake of clarity facts that he, better educated than his supposed audience, could have set forth elsewhere with more subtlety. Though at times casual in his argument, he remains conscious throughout of his commitment to enlightening his fellow citizens.

Rastell's purpose in writing this preface was to explain why the laws should be translated into English. He explains how French came to be the vehicle of English legal parlance. In sweeping generalizations, he recalls how William, duke of Normandy, brought with him his followers. Although they did not understand Anglo-Saxon, William and "other wise men of his Council perceived" that Anglo-Saxon was "homely and rude nor had not so great copy and abundance of words as the French tongue." Neither could the vulgar tongue convey to the French the meanings of the laws they sought implemented. Thus the Normans "ordered, wrote and indited" in French those laws they felt should be made for good governance.

There is more to this seemingly artless survey than is evident from hasty perusal. Inherent in it, for instance, is the patriotism of an Englishman taking a stand against the French. By seeking to rid the law of its French encumbrances, Rastell reveals the depth of his pride in things English. When one considers the bitterness about the French wars Rastell participated in and the patriotic aspects of his printing and exploring activities, it is perhaps fairer to view the preface as expressive of national pride than to focus on the irony which its bland tone at first suggests.

Having dealt with the French involvement in the English legal system, Rastell proceeds to discuss the use of Latin. After William the Conqueror, the French tongue "began to minish," leaving some who understood neither Anglo-Saxon nor French. At this point "the wise men of the realm" agreed that "the English vulgar tongue" would be used for pleading cases and actions and procedures in court, while court records would be kept in Latin, "because that every man generally and indifferently might have knowledge thereof." French, however, remained the tongue for inditing and writing laws.

Such a complicated situation demanded the attention of a wise man, whom Rastell claims Henry VII to have been. This Tudor prince Rastell feels worthy to be called the second Solomon. He perceived the development of the English language through the introduction of translated works and "many noble works" in English. Moreover, increased usage produced a language "amplified and sufficient" to expound laws formerly written in Latin or French. Realizing his subjects "had just pleasure and gave themselves greatly to the reading of the vulgar English tongue," Henry ordained that laws made in his time be in English and "published, declared and imprinted" for better observance. With such an example to emulate, Henry VIII could not but follow in his father's footsteps in this matter.

Rastell's flattery of the Tudors is justified, although possibly motivated more by political than intellectual considerations. Yet the charge of sycophancy is perhaps harsh when one remembers that Rastell was not working for a patron and stood in little danger of having his permission to print these books rejected. What he is doing is expressing his appreciation for rulers who recognized the value in the humanists' endeavor to provide the individual knowledge. The utilization of the vernacular to disseminate knowledge of the law would hasten the advent of that state of tranquillity and peace Rastell so desired.

Rastell's final venture in legal printing was a landmark publication: the first real law dictionary. Entitled *Expositiones Terminorum Legum Anglorum* [Expositions of the terms of the laws of England] (*STC* 10010), the work, probably published in 1525, became popularly known as *Les Termes de la Ley* and was reissued not only by Rastell and his son but by other printers as well. As in his earlier works, Rastell provides a prologue explaining his reasons for this educative task. This prologue, which overstates ideas outlined in his other prefaces, stresses order as the basis of the commonweal. Again, Rastell maintains that the commonweal consists of rule by good laws, but the emphasis now rests upon the good governor whose power and authority must be based on rule of law, and this law must be prescribed. The absence of such a formula results in anarchy. This stress upon common law reveals Rastell's awareness of the individuality of human nature and underscores his commitment to the achievement of freedom for the individual to explore whatever areas he saw fit.

Rastell recognizes the uniqueness of each man. His focus is on the humanity of each man, however lowly his estate. But from this recognition of individuality, Rastell does not proceed to an affirmation of the relativity of morals and laws. For Rastell there can be but one rule of law for all men. If a governor allows each man to live by his own laws, he "bringeth one multitude of people to variance and diversion." These opinions set forth in Rastell's writings of the 1520s contrast noticeably with his Protestant ideas of the next decade, when he streses each man's freedom to live as his conscience dictates. But in 1525, when Rastell wrote his prologue to *Expositiones*, England was yet to embark on its religious rebellion against authority. Law and order were the popular themes of the Tudor regime. The emphasis was on obedience to the law of the prince. Therefore, while Rastell can acknowledge diversity, he advocates that the only equality enjoyed by all is the equality of all men under the rule of good law.

Turning from his philosophy of law to the specific work at hand, Rastell introduces his reasons for publishing his legal dictionary. Just as absence of good law causes wrongs, so does ignorance of the law. A citizenry's ignorance of the law can never be excused except where rulers willfully deter their subjects from acquiring such knowledge. Because law is necessary for the common good, the people must know it to participate in the affairs of the commonweal.

Rastell as a Tudor Humanist

All Rastell's printing in the legal sphere thus can be seen as an outgrowth of his concern for the public to know the laws. A responsible citizen with the means of helping others had a duty to devote his time and talent to the commonweal's betterment. Obviously Rastell took this duty seriously, so seriously that at times he seems self-righteous, even pompous about his importance as an articulate citizen.

At least Rastell was not afraid to act on his convictions. He thought that man could effect change, initiate counsel to improve his country, rejuvenate the legal system through knowledge of laws, raise the level

of life through public education, and increase the international reputation of his country by aiding in economic and political ventures.
Naturally, no one man could effect all these changes; and, if Rastell
thought himself equal to the task, the fault is not in his willingness
to assume such responsibility, but in the reluctance of better qualified
men to share this conception.

G. R. Elton in his *Reform and Renewal* discusses the problem of
translating "bright ideas . . . into action."[18] Most of the English humanist reformers, even More who "should have known better,"
directed their major works at the prince as the source of power to
transform the country. Rastell, however, aimed at a less lofty target,
the average articulate citizen. And ultimately, this practical brand of
applied humanism with its patriotic overtones, even if less sophisticated than the products of the More Circle, was the humanism perhaps destined to be more effective in the long run.

Rastell's Achievement

Although his canon is small, and although he did not concentrate
his literary efforts in one genre, it is difficult not to appreciate his
works. Concentration of effort is not necessarily a virtue, and Rastell's
wide-ranging interests caused him to venture into law, printing, drama,
history, religious controversy, exploration, and many other activities.
Perhaps the most important reason for Rastell's lack of influence as
a literary figure lies in the age itself. The turbulent years of the Reformation failed to provide him with the stable environment so often
needed for the establishment of a literary tradition and cut short what
influence he might have had. As Stanley J. Kahrl observes: "Until
the Elizabethan settlement was secure none of the new directions
pioneered by men like Rastell could develop into modes of expression
capable of stirring audiences throughout England."[19]

A practical-minded man, Rastell, the civic humanist, a thoroughly
middle-class citizen himself, attempted to raise the quality of life in
the English commonwealth by bringing the original and popularized
versions of the more intellectual concerns of his brother-in-law and
others within the grasp of the average man. Hence he directs the
service of his printing press and his works to the educated and un-
educated. He offers a popularized version of Fabyan's history in *The
pastyme* and lessons in natural science in the *Elementis*, so that knowledge which initially reached only a few could become accessible to

many. He seldom doubted the value of common sense, reason, and education, and thought that man could effect change if he was more aware of himself and his place in England, Europe, and the universe. No matter what literary forms they take, such high-minded concerns permeate his works, and his adaptations of the often lofty thoughts of the More Circle and others serve as ways of seeing how he skill-fully reshapes these concepts so they could be understood by far more than he, More, and others ever intended. His inclusion of this goal in almost all he wrote, edited, or printed qualifies much of the criticism leveled at the size of his canon and its lack of concentration in one genre.

His desire to make the English more aware of their heritage as a nation and the position they might attain in western Europe and the newfound lands also motivates much of his writing. Though the *Elementis* develops other subjects, he employs it to tell Englishmen that they should explore the new lands, found colonies in America, and play a role in Western expansion. His universal history, *The pastyme*, displays another facet of his consciousness of England's re-lationship to other nations. Rastell's attempt to expand England's insular mentality extends into foreign literature also, and he encour-ages other literary-minded Englishmen to translate both classical and contemporary treatises, so that the citizenry of the commonweal might partake of the best known and thought throughout the world.

Another aspect unifying Rastell's literary work is his flair for bold experiments. Rastell reshapes traditional forms to fit new ideas into them. The *Elementis* can be seen as a radical attempt to employ the morality form to teach a lesson in geography and natural science. His abbreviation of Fabyan uses a daring typographical arrangement to present his interpretation of historical events. If *Calisto* and *Gentylnes* are his, they also display that willingness to write within a tradition and to depart from it. Even if these literary experiments are not always effective, one must respect the creative imagination which compelled him to attempt what others had not and the often fresh, spontaneous, and entertaining results.

Above all, Rastell's sincere, ever-present hope of serving the com-monweal underlies all his literary works, his other activities, and his life. In almost all he did, regardless of his other motivations, his zealous activism as a citizen of the English commonweal is of ultimate significance.

Notes and References

Chapter One

1. J. D. Mackie, *The Oxford History of England: The Earlier Tudors, 1485–1558* (London: Oxford University Press, 1952), pp. 73, 445–62; E. F. Jacob, *The Oxford History of England: The Fifteenth Century, 1399–1485* (London: Oxford University Press, 1961), pp. 88, 397–401, 513, 547–49, 567–78; A. J. Slavin, *The Precarious Balance: English Government and Society, The Borzoi History of England, 1450–1640*, vol. 3 New York: Knopf, 1973).

2. See pp. l–lii, Mary Dormer Harris, ed., introduction to *The Coventry Leet Book or Mayor's Register*, 4 vols., (London: Kegan Paul, Trench, Trübner, & Co., 1907–13).

3. Harris, *Leet Book*, pp. 128, 156, 158, 165, 174, 201, 202, 204, 207, 211, 236, 247, 256.

4. Harris, *The Register of the Guild of the Holy Trinity, St. Mary, St. John the Baptist, and St. Katherine of Coventry* (London: Oxford University Press, 1935), p. 82, and Jacob, pp. 547–49.

5. Harris, *Leet Book*, pp. 318, 352, 370.

6. H. C. Maxwell Lyte et al., eds., *Calendar of the Patent Rolls, Edward IV, Edward V, and Richard III* (London, 1901), p. 576; A. W. Reed, *Early Tudor Drama: Medwall, the Rastells, Heywood, and the More Circle* (London, 1926), p. 1; hereafter cited as *ETD*.

7. E. Gordon Duff, *The Printers, Stationers and Bookbinders of Westminster and London from 1476 to 1535* (London: Cambridge University Press, 1906), p. 183.

8. John Pits, *Relatio Historicarum de Rebus Anglicis* (Paris, 1619), p. 724.

9. Reed, *ETD*, p. 2.

10. Lyte et al., eds. *Calendar of the Patent Rolls, Henry VII, 1494–1509*, vol. 2 (London, 1916), pp. 395, 419, 604.

11. Harris, *Leet Book*, pp. 603–5, 619.

12. See the introduction to the Rastell selections by Elizabeth M. Nugent, ed., *The Thought and Culture of the English Renaissance: An Anthology of Tudor Prose, 1481–1555* (London: Cambridge University Press, 1956), p. 167.

13. Reed, *ETD*, pp. 3, 6. See Reed's chapter in F. J. C. Hearnshaw, ed., *The Social and Political Ideas of Some Great Thinkers of the Renais-*

sance and the Reformation (New York: Barnes and Noble, 1949), pp. 123–48.

14. Hearnshaw, p. 130.

15. Reed, *ETD*, p. 2, citing Public Record Office (hereafter cited as PRO), *King's Book of Payments*, E. 415/31 (f. 20).

16. David Quinn, "John Rastell," *Dictionary of Canadian Biography*, vol. 1 (Toronto: University of Toronto Press, 1966), pp. 565–66; Reed, *ETD*, p. 2; Geritz, "The Marriage Date of John Rastell and Elizabeth More," *Moreana* 52 (1976):23–24.

17. Reed, *ETD*, p. 225; see app. 7, pp. 224–29.

18. See Pearl Hogrefe, *The Sir Thomas More Circle: A Program of Ideas and Their Impact on Secular Drama* (Urbana, 1959).

19. See Reed, *ETD*, p. xi, and Hogrefe, p. 196.

20. Charles Phythian-Adams, *Desolation of a City: Coventry and the Urban Crisis of the Late Middle Ages* (Cambridge: Cambridge University Press, 1979), pp. 38, 281–82.

21. Reed, *ETD*, p. 4.

22. J. S. Brewer, James Gardiner, and R. H. Brodie, eds., *Letters and Papers: Foreign and Domestic of the Reign of Henry VIII* (London: Longman, 1862–1920), vol. 1, pt. 2, p. 1476; hereafter cited as *L & P*.

23. Ibid., p. 1482.

24. Hogrefe, p. 110.

25. Preserved Smith, *The Age of Reformation* (New York: Henry Holt & Co., 1920), p. 537; see also Elizabeth L. Eisenstein, *The Printing Press as an Agent of Change* (New York: Cambridge University Press, 1979), pp. 22–23.

26. Russell Ames, *Citizen Thomas More and His Utopia* (Princeton: Princeton University Press, 1949), pp. 103–4.

27. Sylvia L. Thrupp, *The Merchant Class of Medieval London* (Ann Arbor: University of Michigan Press, 1948), pp. 157–63.

28. Colin Clair, *A History of Printing in Britain* (New York: Oxford University Press, 1966), pp. 1–4; H. S. Bennett, *English Books and Readers, 1475 to 1557: Being a Study in the History of the Book Trade from Caxton to the Incorporation of the Stationers' Company* (London: Cambridge University Press, 1952), p. 30.

29. Clair, p. 2; Eisenstein, p. 392.

30. *An abridgment of statutes* (London, 1519).

31. David Cressey, *Literacy and the Social Order: Reading and Writing in Tudor and Stuart England* (Cambridge: University Press, 1980), pp. 13, 44.

32. See also *The English Works of Thomas More in 2 Volumes*, ed. and intro. by W. E. Campbell and A. W. Reed (London: Eyre and Spottiswoode, 1931), 1:18—cited hereafter as *More Works*. Frank Isaac in

English and Scottish Printing Types: (1501–35)—(1508–41) (London: Oxford University Press, 1930), p. 36, cites the "flete bryde" as the first of three printing sites used by Rastell.

33. Isaac, p. 36.

34. E. Gordon Duff, *A Century of the English Book Trade: Short Notices of all Printers, Stationers, Bookbinders, and others connected with it from the issue of the first dated book in 1457 to the Incorporation of the Company of Stationers in 1557* (London: Bibliographical Society, 1905), p. xvii.

35. The depositions from Court of Chancery from 26 Henry 8 (1534–35), made in connection with Rastell's printing house, "the Mermaid next Paul's Gate," are reprinted by Henry Robert Plomer in "John Rastell and his Contemporaries," *Bibliographica* 2 (1896):437–51; Reed, *ETD*, p. 18.

36. Clair, p. 45.

37. Duff, p. 184.

38. Plomer discusses some of these men in his article, 448–49. See also R. J. Roberts, "John Rastell's Inventory of 1538," *Library*, 6th ser. 1, no. 1 (1979):34–42.

39. Reed, *ETD*, p. 112; Bennett, p. 209.

40. *Progymnasmata grammatices vulgaria* (*STC* 15635).

41. Hugh William Davies, *Devices of the Early Printers, 1475–1560: Their History and Development with a Chapter on Portrait Figures of Printers* (London: Grafton and Co., 1935), pp. 356–58.

42. Duff, p. xviii.

43. Plomer, *A Short History of English Printing, 1476–1898* (London: Kegan Paul, Trench, Trübner, and Co., 1900), p. 52; Hogrefe, p. 28.

44. Plomer, *Printing*, p. 51.

45. Ibid., p. 52.

46. Reed, *ETD*, p. 8; Joseph Henry Beale, *A Bibliography of Early English Law Books* (Cambridge: Harvard University Press, 1926), p. 190; Plomer, *Printing*, p. 53.

47. Plomer, *Bibliographica*, 441; Isaac, p. 38.

48. Robert Steele, *The Earliest English Music Printing: A Description and Bibliography of English Printed Music to the Close of the Sixteenth Century* (London: Chiswick Press, 1903), pp. 1–5.

49. Alexander Hyatt King, *Four Hundred Years of Music Printing* (London: Eyre and Spottiswoode, 1964), pp. 15–16; see also King's "The Significance of John Rastell in Early Music Printing," *Library* 5th ser., 26 (1971):197–214.

50. Both are in the British Library and have been tentatively assigned to the years immediately after 1525. See King, *Four Hundred*, p. 16.

51. The British Library fragment has the catalog entry, "perhaps written by Rastell, the printer" (London, 1520?).

52. Its date is still disputed, though it seems to be around 1525. The song is printed on sigs. E5, E6, E6^v; the words themselves appear on E8. See Percy M. Young, *A History of British Music* (New York: W. W. Norton & Co., 1967), p. 117.

53. *STC* 5892; see Steele, p. 5.

54. *STC* 23145 gives this information about the only existing copy at Oxford.

55. Ray Nash, "Rastell Fragments at Dartmouth," *Library* 4th ser., 24 (1943–44):69–70.

56. With a suggested date of 1530.

57. See Joseph Ames, *Typographical Antiquities or The History of Printing in England, Scotland, and Ireland: Containing Memoirs of our Ancient Printers and a Register of the Books Printed by Them*, aug. William Herbert and ed. Thomas Dibdin (London: W. Blumer & Co., 1816), 3:99.

58. *STC* 17327 assigns a date of 1530. When published, volume 1 of the new edition of the *STC* should clarify some of these problems.

59. See Nash's article.

60. Only two leaves are extant of the edition printed probably in 1525.

61. See Joseph Ames, p. 98.

62. See E. E. Reynolds, *Thomas More and Erasmus* (New York: Fordham University Press, 1965), p. 77.

63. Isaac, p. 36.

64. Stanley J. Kahrl, "The Medieval Origins of the Sixteenth-Century English Jest-books," *Studies in the Renaissance* 13 (1966):166.

65. P. M. Zall, ed., *A Hundred Merry Tales and Other English Jest-books of the Fifteenth and Sixteenth Centuries* (Lincoln: University of Nebraska Press, 1963), p. 1.

66. "Emprynted at London at the sygne of the mere-mayde at Pollis gate next to chepe syde, 23 March MCXXXV." Reprinted by W. Carew Hazlitt in *Old English Jest Books or Shakespeare's Jest Books*, vol. 3 (London, 1864); Reed, *ETD*, p. 47.

67. Plomer, *Bibliographica*, 442.

68. Zall, p. 58; Herman Oesterley published a copy of the *Tales* in *Shakespeare's Jest Book or A Hundred Mery Talys* (London: John Russell Smith, 1866).

69. Zall, pp. 6–8.

70. See Reynolds, chap. 17. *STC* incorrectly lists William Rastell as printer. The colophon is John Rastell's; and, although the son was work-

ing with his father and later published another edition of the work, the father was the original publisher.

71. Reed, *ETD*, pp. 75–76.

72. For the Hunne story see A. G. Dickens, *The English Reformation* (London: B. T. Batsford, 1964), pp. 90–96, and G. R. Elton, *Reform and Reformation: England, 1509–1558* (Cambridge: Harvard University Press, 1977), pp. 51–58.

73. Reed, *ETD*, pp. 9–10. Reed also mentions this fact in his introduction to *More Works*, 2:6–7.

74. E. M. G. Routh, *Sir Thomas More and His Friends, 1477–1535* (New York: Russell and Russell, 1963), pp. 43–44.

75. Reed, *ETD*, p. 10.

76. *L & P*, vol. 2, pt. 2, p. 960; reprinted in James A. Williamson, *The Voyages of the Cabots and English Discovery of North America under Henry VII and Henry VIII* (London: Argonaut Press, 1929), pp. 85–86. See E. J. Devereux, "John Rastell's Utopian Voyage," *Moreana* 51 (September 1976):119–23.

77. Reprinted in Reed, *ETD*, pp. 187–201, and explained in Williamson, pp. 244–48.

78. Reed, *ETD*, p. 12; Tryggvi J. Oleson, *Early Voyages and Northern Approaches, 1000–1632* (Toronto: McClelland and Stewart, 1963), pp. 145–46.

79. See Reed, *ETD*, p. 202.

80. See Sydney Anglo, *Spectacle, Pageantry, and Early Tudor Policy* (Oxford, 1969), pp. 164–67, 262–65.

81. *L & P*, vol. 3, pt. 1, pp. 259–67.

82. An item in Town Clerk's records 5 May as cited by Reed, *John Heywood and His Friends* (London: Alexander Moring, 1917), pp. 22–23; Anglo, pp. 196–97; Routh, p. 113; Mackie, pp. 306–8.

83. Edward Hall, *The Union of the Two Noble and Illustre Famelies of Lancastre and Yorke . . .* (1548; reprint ed., London: G. Woodfall, 1809), p. 637.

84. Hall, p. 640.

85. Anglo, p. 197.

86. *L & P*, vol. 3, pt. 2, p. 1285.

87. Reed, *ETD*, pp. 14–16.

88. *L & P*, vol. 3, pt. 2, pp. 1367, 1371; vol. 4, pt. 1, p. 238.

89. Reed, *ETD*, pp. 16, 230–31.

90. Ibid., p. 17.

91. This lawsuit is published by Plomer as "Pleadings in a Theatrical Lawsuit. From the Records of the Court of Requests. John Rastell *v.* Henry Walton," in *An English Garner: Fifteenth Century Prose and*

Verse, ed. A. W. Pollard (London: Archibald Constable and Co., 1903), 1:307–21; hereafter cited as Plomer, *Garner*.

92. Reed, *ETD*, p. 21.

93. Plomer, *Garner*, p. 318.

94. Ibid., pp. 307–8.

95. Ibid., 316; Reed, *ETD*, p. 233.

96. Plomer, *Garner*, p. 315.

97. *L & P*, vol. 4, pt. 2, p. 1395.

98. See Anglo, pp. 212–25; *L & P*, vol. 4, pt. 2, pp. 1394–95; Reed, *ETD*, p. 18.

99. Hall, p. 723.

100. *L & P*, vol. 4, pt. 2, p. 1396; Anglo, pp. 221–22.

101. Reed, *ETD*, p. 20.

102. *L & P*, vol. 4, pt. 1, p. 752.

103. *L & P*, vol. 4, pt. 2, pp. 2171–72, 2215; pt. 3, p. 2547.

104. Ibid., pt. 3, p. 2692. See also Standford E. Lehmberg, *The Reformation Parliament, 1520–1526* (London: Cambridge University Press, 1970), pp. 29–31, 121–22.

105. Thomas Fuller, *The Worthies of England*, ed. John Freeman (London: George Allen and Unwin, 1952), p. 355.

106. Thomas Russell, ed., *The Works of the English and Scottish Reformers*, vol. 4 (London: S. & R. Bentley, 1829), p. 211; Fuller, p. 355.

107. *More Works*, 1:4.

108. *L & P*, 6:132–33. See Reed, *ETD*, p. 22.

109. Ibid., 6:660–61.

110. Ibid., p. 6:489. In the same volume, p. 581, the Dartmouth Forest grant appears a second time.

111. *L & P*, 7:597.

112. Ibid., 8:40, 47.

113. Ibid., 7:452.

114. Ibid., 7:364.

115. Reed, *ETD*, p. 23.

116. *L & P*, 8:56.

117. Ibid., 9:78.

118. Ibid., 10:531.

119. Ibid., 7:417; PRO, London, *State Papers*, 1, vol. 85, item 129.

120. PRO, *State Papers*, 1, vol. 85, item 130. See also *L & P*, 7:417–18.

121. PRO, *State Papers*, 1, vol. 85, items 131–32; see also *L & P*, 7:418. Further references will be to the reprint (except where the original has been omitted) in Sir Henry Ellis, *Original Letters Illustrative of English History Including Numerous Royal Letters*, 3d ser., 2 (London: S. & J. Bentley, Wilson, & Frey, 1846), pp. 308–12.

122. Ellis, pp. 309–10.

123. Reed, *ETD*, p. 24.

124. Ellis, p. 310.

125. Duff, p. 185.

126. Ellis, pp. 310–11.

127. Ibid., p. 311.

128. Ibid., p. 312.

129. *L & P*, 7:345, 354; Reed, *ETD*, p. 25.

130. Ibid., 8:293.

131. Ibid., 8:227.

132. Ibid., 10, p. 90; Reed, *ETD*, pp. 26, 115; Reed, *John Heywood*, p. 35.

133. PRO, *State Papers,* 1, vol. 113, item 219. See also *L & P*, 11:585.

134. All further references are to the copy of the will on file in Somerset House, London (B.M. 3 Crumwell).

135. Duff, p. 185.

136. Reed, *ETD*, pp. 27, 84; Reed, *John Heywood*, p. 57.

137. *L & P*, 11:718.

138. Ibid., 11:506–8.

Chapter Two

1. All parenthetical references to the *Elementis, Calisto,* and *Gentylnes* are to Richard Axton's edition (Totowa, N.J., 1979).

2. Reed, *ETD*, p. 12.

3. Ibid., pp. 104–17; Hogrefe, pp. 262–74; 300–301.

4. See Williamson, pp. 88, 246.

5. Johnstone Parr, "John Rastell's Geographical Knowledge of America," *PQ* 27 (July 1948):231–32.

6. See Reed, *ETD*, p. 106; Charles R. Baskervill, "John Rastell's Dramatic Activities," *MP* 13 (1916):559; Esther C. Dunn, "John Rastell and 'Gentleness and Nobility'," *MLR* 12 (1917):266–78, and Richard Southern, *The Staging of Plays Before Shakespeare* (London, 1973), pp. 204–16.

7. David Bevington, *From Mankind to Marlowe: Growth of Structure in the Popular Drama of Tudor England* (Cambridge, Mass., 1962), pp. 46–47.

8. All references to *Fulgens* and *Nature* are taken from the edition of Alan H. Nelson (Totowa, N.J., Rowman and Littlefield, 1980).

9. E. Hamilton Moore, *English Miracle Plays and Moralities* (1907; reprint ed., New York: AMS Press, 1969), p. 144.

10. See Roger Coleman's remarks about cutting in his edition of the play (Cambridge: University Printhouse, 1971) and Axton, p. 125, F. vi.

11. Robert L. Ramsey, Introduction to his edition of *Magnyfycence, A*

Moral Play (London: Kegan Paul, Trench, Trübner & Co., 1907), pp. cxlvii–clxxiii.

12. Axton, pp. 11–12.

13. See J. E. Bernard, Jr., *The Prosody of the Tudor Interlude* (New Haven, 1939), pp. 28–29; Ramsey, pp. cxxxiv–cxlvii, and Axton, pp. 12–14.

14. Moore, p. 175.

15. Ramsey, pp. clxxiii–cxcvii.

16. Axton, p. 12.

17. Hogrefe, pp. 267–68.

18. M. E. Borish, "Source and Intention of *The Four Elements*," *SP* 35 (April 1938):150.

19. Ramsey, p. clxxx.

20. From 1938 to 1948, several articles investigated the sources of Rastell's scientific and geographical information. For the most part, they concluded his knowledge was dated, incomplete, and inaccurate. Parr and Hogrefe, however, have demonstrated the opposite viewpoint.

21. Hogrefe, pp. 262–74.

22. Ibid., p. 265.

23. W. W. Greg, *A Bibliography of the English Printed Drama to the Restoration* (London: Oxford University Press, 1939), 1:87.

24. Axton, p. 15.

25. See Reed, *ETD*, pp. 52, 110–16; Baskervill, "Rastell's Dramatic Activities," 557–60; F. S. Boas, *An Introduction to Tudor Drama* (Oxford: Clarendon Press, 1933), p. 9; Kenneth Walter Cameron, *Authorship and Sources of "Gentleness and Nobility"* (Raleigh, N.C., 1941), pp. 69–70, 73–75; Hogrefe, pp. 340, 344–45; Rosenbach, "The Influence of 'The Celestina' in Early English Drama," *Jahrbuch der Deutschen Shakespeare-Gesellschaft* 39 (1903):43–61; Robert Carl Johnson, *John Heywood* (New York: Twayne Publishers, 1970), p. 127, and Gustav Ungerer, *Anglo-Spanish Relations in Tudor Literature* (Bern, 1956) for discussion of the authorship question.

26. Boies Penrose, *Travel and Discovery in the Renaissance, 1420–1620* (Cambridge: Harvard University Press, 1952), p. 313.

27. All references to *La Celestina*, except when noted otherwise, are to the James Mabbe translation (1631), in *Tudor Translations* (New York, 1967), a reprint of James Fitzmaurice-Kelly's edition (London, 1894).

28. Mack H. Singleton, trans., *La Celestina* (Madison: University of Wisconsin Press, 1958); these lines follow the prologue and precede the "summary of the whole work."

29. H. Warner Allen, *An Interlude of Calisto and Melebea for the First Time Accurately Reproduced from the Original Copy, Printed by*

John Rastell, c. 1530. Celestina, or the Tragi-Comedy of Calisto and Melebea, Trans. from Spanish by James Mabbe, anno 1631 (London, 1908), p. 341.

30. See H. D. Purcell's "The *Celestina* and the *Interlude of Calisto and Melebea*," *BHS* 44 (1967):1–15, in which the author maintains that Calisto's author also uses parts of act 6 and the prologue of the original.

31. Rosenbach, p. 51.

32. Fitzmaurice-Kelly, p. xxxv.

33. Rosenbach, p. 50.

34. Allen, p. 332.

35. Ibid., p. 333.

36. Axton, pp. 17–18.

37. Hogrefe, pp. 339–44; see also Richard Allen Pacholski's dissertation, "The Humanist Drama of the Sir Thomas More Circle" (University of Wisconsin-Madison, 1969).

38. Allen, p. 345.

39. Rosenbach, p. 54.

40. See Jill Mann's *Chaucer and Medieval Estates Satire: The Literature of Social Classes and the General Prologue to The Canterbury Tales* (Cambridge: At the University Press, 1973), p. 3 for valuable generalizations about these topics.

41. See Pollard's "Critical Essay" in C. M. Gayley's edition of *Representative Comedies* (New York: The Macmillan Co., 1916), 1:8–9; Baskervill, "John Rastell and 'Gentleness and Nobility,'" *MLR* 12 (1917):266–78; Reed, *ETD*, pp. 107–12; and Joel B. Altman, *The Tudor Play of Mind: Rhetorical Inquiry and the Development of Elizabethan Drama* (Berkeley, 1978), pp. 26, 124–29.

42. Cameron, p. 88. Interestingly enough, Cameron argues that some of the play's ideas are exclusively Heywoodian—the very premise of some who support Rastell's claim as author. See also G. F. Tucker Brooke, *The Tudor Drama* (Boston: Houghton Mifflin, 1911), p. 95, and his "Authorship and Sources of 'Gentleness and Nobility,'" *MLR* 6 (1911): 458–61; R. W. Bolwell, *The Life and Works of John Heywood* (New York: Columbia University Press, 1921), p. 93; Cameron, pp. 59–89; and Johnson, pp. 120–27.

43. Axton, pp. 20–21.

44. Bevington, *Tudor Drama and Politics: A Critical Approach to Topical Meaning* (Cambridge, Mass., 1968), pp. 76–81.

45. Altman, p. 125.

46. Ibid., p. 129.

47. Hogrefe, p. 287; Bevington, *Tudor Drama*, p. 78.

48. See Axton, p. 23 for the long literary tradition behind the Plowman's character.

49. Hogrefe, pp. 285, 287; Bevington, *Tudor Drama*, p. 77.

50. See Pacholski's chapter on *Gentylnes*.

51. Altman, p. 129.

Chapter Three

1. Plomer, *Printing*, p. 53.

2. The British Library possesses this copy bought in 1773 from the estate of James West who received the book in 1760 from the earl of Oxford.

3. London, 1811; hereafter cited as *Pastyme* in the notes or by the page in the text.

4. F. J. Levy, *Tudor Historical Thought* (San Marino, 1967), p. 73.

5. Plomer, *Bibliographica*, 445.

6. Joseph Ames, p. 92.

7. See Anglo, chap. 4.

8. Plomer, *Bibliographica*, 445.

9. See King, "Early Music Printing," pp. 197–214.

10. Arthur B. Ferguson, *Clio Unbound: Perception of the Social and Cultural Past in Renaissance England* (Durham: Duke University Press, 1979), p. 4.

11. Levy, p. xi.

12. See Levy and Ferguson, "Circumstances and Sense of History in Tudor England," *Medieval and Renaissance Studies* 3 (1968):170–205; T. D. Kendrick, *British Antiquity* (London: Methuen and Co., 1950); and F. Smith Fussner, *Tudor History and the Historians* (New York: Basic Books, 1970), pp. 6–7.

13. See Anglo, "The *British History* in Early Tudor Propaganda," *Bulletin of the John Rylands Library* 44, no. 1 (1961):17–48.

14. See Kendrick, pp. 4 ff., 89 ff., 101 ff.

15. Ibid., pp. 15, 39.

16. See Levy, pp. 10–16.

17. Kendrick, pp. 13–14.

18. See Dibdin's introduction to the *Pastyme*, p. vii, and John Taylor, ed., *The Universal Chronicle of Ranulf Higden* (Oxford: Clarendon Press, 1966).

19. See Levy, pp. 19–21; all references to Fabyan are taken from Henry Ellis, ed., *The New Chronicles of England and France in Two Parts* (London: G. Woodfall, 1811)—hereafter cited as Fabyan in notes or by page in the text.

20. Reed, *ETD*, p. 79. Mackie, p. 580, incorrectly says Rastell printed this edition.

21. *Pastyme*, p. 96; here Rastell is following Fabyan's criticism, pp. 41–42.

22. *Pastyme*, p. 135, omits Canute and the tide story found in Fabyan, p. 219.

23. Compare *Pastyme*, pp. 292–99 and Fabyan, pp. 670–73. See More, *The History of King Richard the Third*, in *The Complete Works of St. Thomas More*, vol. 2, ed. R. S. Sylvester, (New Haven: Yale University Press, 1963), pp. 265–66.

24. Reed, *ETD*, p. 214.

25. See ibid., pp. 106–7.

26. See *Pastyme*, pp. 129–31 for one such example. See also Franklin Le Van Baumer, *The Early Tudor Theory of Kingship* (New York: Russell and Russell, 1966).

27. Ferguson, "Circumstances," 188.

28. Kendrick, p. 34.

29. See ibid., pp. 36–41; Ferguson, *The Indian Summer of English Chivalry* (Durham: Duke University Press, 1960), pp. 84–103.

30. Kendrick, p. 83.

31. Levy, p. 73.

32. *Pastyme*, p. 6; see Levy, p. 73.

33. *Pastyme*, pp. 4–5; Nugent, *The Thought and the Culture*, pp. 503–9.

34. George B. Parks, "Rastell and Waldseemüller's Map," *PMLA* 48 (1943):572–74.

35. *Pastyme*, pp. 5–7, 87–88; Fabyan, pp. 8–11.

36. Fabyan, pp. 79–81; *Pastyme*, pp. 106–7.

37. Kendrick, pp. 95–96.

38. Levy, p. 74.

39. Kendrick, p. 41.

40. Ferguson, "Circumstances," p. 171.

41. All references to *A Supplication* are taken from the revised 1529 edition of Frederick J. Furnival (London: Kegan Paul, Trench, Trübner, & Co., 1871).

42. Nugent, *The Thought and the Culture*, p. 215. See Dickens, *The English Reformation*, pp. 28, 69, 91–94, 100, 326 for a complete account of the Hunne case.

43. C. S. Lewis, *English Literature in the Sixteenth Century Excluding Drama* (Oxford: Clarendon Press, 1954), p. 196.

44. All references to More's *Supplication of Souls* are from Sister Mary Thecla's edition (Westminster, Md.: Newman Press, 1950).

45. See Rainer Pineas, *Thomas More and Tudor Polemics* (Bloomington: Indiana University Press, 1968), pp. 61–81.

46. Ferguson, *The Articulate Citizen and the English Renaissance* (Durham: Duke University Press, 1965), p. 220.

47. Dickens, pp. 104–8.

48. All references to *A new boke of Purgatory* are taken from the British Library copy.

49. Lewis, p. 196.

50. Ibid.

51. This page was numbered D4 in error; it really is D3.

52. This page is incorrectly numbered D4ᵛ; it should be D3ᵛ.

53. E. J. Devereux, "John Rastell's Press in the English Reformation," *Moreana* 49 (1976):29–47.

54. All references to Frith's works are taken from *The Works of the English and Scottish Reformers*, ed. Thomas Russell, (London: n.p., 1829).

55. Marcus L. Loane, *Pioneers of the Reformation in England* (London: Church Book Room Press, 1964), p. 12.

56. Foxe, *The Acts and Monuments of John Foxe*, ed. Stephen Reed Cattley, vol. 5 (London: Religious Tract Society, 1838), p. 9.

57. Reed, *ETD*, p. 221.

Chapter Four

1. Boas, *An Introduction to Tudor Drama*, pp. 9–10.

2. Baskervill, "John Rastell's Dramatic Activities," p. 560.

3. Hogrefe, p. 130; Elton, *Reform and Renewal: Thomas Cromwell and the Commonwealth* (London: Cambridge University Press, 1973), pp. 63 ff. relates the influence of the More Circle upon Tudor government.

4. Bennett, *English Books, 1475*, p. 7, and Dunn, "John Rastell and 'Gentleness and Nobility,'" p. 273.

5. See the introduction to Rastell's works in Nugent's *The Thought and the Culture*, p. 168.

6. Hogrefe, p. 130, and Elton, *The Tudor Constitution: Documents and Commentary* (London: Cambridge University Press, 1960), p. 147.

7. Baumer, pp. 160–61.

8. Bennett, *English Books and Readers, 1558–1603: Being a Study in the History of the Book Trade in the Reign of Elizabeth I* (London: Cambridge University Press, 1965), pp. 156–57.

9. William S. Holdsworth, *A History of English Law*, 4th ed. (London: n.p., 1936), 2:460, and F. W. Maitland, *Year Books of Edward III*, vol. 17 (London: Selden Society, 1903), p. ix. See also Bennett, *English Books, 1475*, pp. 81–82.

10. All pagination, whether in the text or notes, refers to the Nugent

version, pp. 169–73. See also Howard Jay Graham, "The Rastells and the Printed English Law Book of the Renaissance," *Law Library Journal* 47 (1954):6–25.

11. Nugent, p. 170.

12. Ibid., p. 171.

13. Ibid.

14. *Tabula prime partis magni abbreviamenti librorum legum anglorum* (*STC* 10955). See Graham and John W. Heckel, "The Book that 'Made' the Common Law: The First Printing of Fitzherbert's 'La Graunde Abridgment,' 1514–1516," *Law Library Journal* 51 (1958):100–116.

15. See Gordon Zeeveld's introductory essay, "Political and Social Order," in Nugent, pp. 159–67. Also illuminating is Ferguson, *Articulate Citizen*, chap. 6, and Slavin, *Precarious Balance*, chap. 3.

16. The preface as printed by Nugent, pp. 173–76, a reprint of the 1527 (*STC* 1518) of the 1519 original, is used. See also the reprint in Graham's " 'Our Tong Maternall Marvellously Amendyd and Augmentyd': The First Englishing and Printing of the Medieval Statutes at Large, 1530–1533," *UCLA Law Review* 13 (November 1965):58–98.

17. Reed, *ETD*, p. 204.

18. Elton, p. 66.

19. Stanley J. Kahrl, *Traditions of Medieval English Drama* (Pittsburgh: University of Pittsburgh Press, 1975), p. 123.

Selected Bibliography

PRIMARY SOURCES

1. Important Editions

Authorship and Sources of "Gentleness and Nobility": A Study in Early Tudor Drama Together with a Text of the Play Based on the Black-Letter Original. Edited by Kenneth Walter Cameron. Raleigh, N.C.: Thistle Press, 1941. Provides information on nobility in medieval-Renaissance literature and a carefully edited text.

Das "Interlude of the Four Elements" mit einer ien leitung neu her ausgegeben in marburger studien gur englischen philogie. Edited by Julius Fischer. Marburg: N. G. Elwert, 1903. Standard, most scholarly, edition, preserving spelling found in the Garrick collection copy in British Library; introduction speculates on composition, date, and relationship to *Nature.*

An Interlude of Calisto and Melebea for the First Time Accurately Reproduced from the Original Copy, Printed by John Rastell, c. 1530, Celestina or the Tragi-Comedy of Calisto and Melebea, Trans. from Spanish by James Mabbe, anno. 1631. Edited by H. Warner Allen. London: G. Routledge, 1908. Contains notes and introductions to *Calisto* assessing the *Celestina's* place in English literature.

The Pastime of People. Edited by T. F. Dibdin. London, 1811. Adequate edition reorders Rastell's typographical arrangement.

Three Rastell Plays. Edited by Richard Axton. Totowa, N.J.: Rowman and Littlefield, 1979. Texts presented in old-spelling based on originals, with notes, glosses, and introductions.

2. Other Editions

Gentleness and Nobility. Edited by John S. Farmer. Tudor Facsimile Text. Amersham, England, 1914.

————. Edited by A. C. Partridge and F. P. Wilson. Oxford: Oxford University Press, 1949. Facsimile.

The Interlude of Calisto and Melebea. Edited by W. W. Greg and Frank Sidgwick. Oxford: Malone Society Reprints, 1908. Facsimile.

The Interlude of the Four Elements. Edited by James O. Halliwell. Early English Poetry, Ballads, and Popular Literature of the Middle Ages, vol. 22. London: Richards, 1848.

John Rastell: The Four Elements as Performed at the University Printing House, Cambridge, in the Summer of this Year Now, Printed for

Friends at Christmas, 1971. Edited by Roger Coleman. Cambridge: University Printing House, 1971. Illustrated version as performed.

The Nature of the Four Elements. Edited by John S. Farmer. Tudor Facsimile Text. London, 1908.

A Selection of Old English Plays Originally Published by Robert Dodsley in the Year 1744. Vol. 1. Edited by W. Carew Hazlitt. London: Reeves and Turner, 1874. Reprints *The Four Elementis* and *Calisto*.

Six Anonymous Plays, First Series (c. 1510–1537), Early English Dramatists. Edited by John S. Farmer. London: Early English Drama Society, 1905.

The Spider and the Fly Together with an Attributed Interlude Entitled Gentleness and Nobility by John Heywood. Edited by John S. Farmer. London: Early English Drama Society, 1908.

SECONDARY SOURCES

1. Bibliographies

Geritz, Albert J. "Recent Studies in John Rastell." *English Literary Renaissance* 8 (1978):341–50. Lists over 350 entries, annotates some, and attempts to be exhaustive through 1975.

Houle, Peter J. *The English Morality and Related Drama: A Bibliography*. Hamden, Conn.: Archon Books, 1972. Includes entries pertaining to Rastell; no annotations.

Stratman, Carl J. *A Bibliography of Medieval Drama*. Los Angeles: University of California Press, 1954. Contains entries on Rastell; no annotations.

2. Books and Parts of Books

Altman, Joel. *The Tudor Play of Mind: Rhetorical Inquiry and the Development of Elizabethan Drama*. Berkeley: University of California Press, 1978. Comments on *Gentylnes* provide new avenues of interpretation.

Anglo, Sydney. *Spectacle, Pageantry, and Early Tudor Policy*. Oxford: Clarendon Press, 1969. Mentions Rastell's role in designing three spectacles of Henry VIII's reign.

Berdan, John M. *Early Tudor Poetry: 1485–1547*. New York: Macmillan Co., 1939. Pioneer study discusses influences of Spanish literature on Tudor writers.

Bernard, J. E., Jr. *The Prosody of the Tudor Interlude*. New Haven: Yale University Press, 1939. Analyzes prosody of three Rastell plays.

Bevington, David. *From Mankind to Marlowe*. Cambridge: Harvard University Press, 1962. Notes the schoolmaster stance of *The Four Ele-*

mentis and its attempt to improve the populace by using common language.

―――. *Tudor Drama and Politics: A Critical Approach to Topical Meaning.* Cambridge: Harvard University Press, 1968. Considers *The Four Elementis*, *Calisto*, and *Gentylnes* as manifestos of social, political, economic movements.

Fitzmaurice-Kelly, J. *The Relations Between Spanish and English Literature.* Liverpool: At the University Press, 1910. Condemns *Calisto*'s ending for its alteration of its source.

Hogrefe, Pearl. *The Sir Thomas More Circle: A Program of Ideas and Their Impact on Secular Drama.* Urbana: University of Illinois Press, 1959. Calls Rastell the most energetic dramatist of the More Circle, draws attention to Finsbury Fields stage, discusses *The Four Elementis*, *Calisto*, and *Gentylnes*, and shows interest in Rastell's civic concerns.

Levy, F. J. *Tudor Historical Thought.* San Marino, Calif.: Huntington Library, 1967. Examines *The pastyme*'s typographical arrangement as expression of Rastell's skeptical attitude toward historical veracity.

Reed, A. W. *Early Tudor Drama: Medwall, The Rastells, Heywood, and The More Circle.* London: Muethen and Co., 1926. Breaks ground for exploration of Rastell and provides appendices of essential documents.

Schelling, F. E. *Foreign Influences in Elizabethan Plays.* New York: Harper & Brothers, 1923. Finds characters, dialogue, structure, and plot of *Calisto* unusual for an interlude.

Southern, Richard. *The Staging of Plays Before Shakespeare.* London: Faber & Faber, 1973. Discusses cutting *The Four Elementis* and its costumes, song, and dance; provides a sketch of a scene depicting its schoolmaster stance.

Ungerer, Gustav. *Anglo-Spanish Relations in Tudor Literature.* Swiss Studies in English, vol. 38. Bern: Francke Verlag, 1956. Considers *Celestina*'s influence on *Calisto*; utilizes word choices and usage patterns characteristic of Rastell's known works to substantiate authorship.

3. Articles

Baskervill, C. R. "John Rastell's Dramatic Activities." *MP* 13 (1916): 557–60. Uses parallel passages to demonstrate *Calisto*, *Gentylnes*, and *Necromantia* are Rastell's works.

Borish, M. E. "Source and Intention of *The Four Elementis*." *SP* 35 (1938):149–63. Maintains this interlude attempts not only to interest Englishmen in exploration but also the best Continental learning on cosmography.

Devereux, E. J. "John Rastell's Press in the English Reformation." *Moreana* 49 (1976):29–47. Examines the consequences of involvement in religious controversy.

————. "John Rastell's Text of the *Parliament of Fowls*." *Moreana* 27 (1970):115–20. Conjectures copy from which the poem was set was riddled with errors, and that Rastell may have corrupted the text for propriety's sake.

Ferguson, Arthur B. "Circumstances and Sense of History in Tudor England." *Journal of Medieval and Renaissance Studies* 3 (1968):170–205. Explores Rastell's skeptical attitude toward the historical validity of legends as efforts to apply modern scholarly standards to pseudohistory.

King, A. Hyatt. "The Significance of John Rastell in Early Music Printing." *Library*, 5th ser., 26 (1971):197–214. Credits Rastell as printer-editor of earliest mensural music in England, earliest broadside ballad in Europe, and earliest song in English drama.

Nash, Ray. "Rastell Fragments at Dartmouth." *Library* 24 (1944):66–73. Raises further questions about canon.

Nugent, Elizabeth M. "Sources of John Rastell's *The Nature of the Four Elementis*." *PMLA* 57 (1942):74–88. Argues Rastell consulted contemporary cosmology and voyages.

Parks, George B. "Rastell and Waldseemüller's Map." *PMLA* 58 (1943): 572–74. Declares Rastell's knowledge of geography and natural science was not thorough.

Parr, Johnstone. "More Sources of *Rastell's Interlude of the Four Elementis*." *PMLA* 60 (1945):48–58. Adds scholarly and popular sources.

————. "John Rastell's Geographical Knowledge of America." *PQ* 27 (1948): 229–40. Claims Rastell's geography is as accurate as one could expect from a well-read man of the sixteenth century.

Plomer, Henry B. "John Rastell and his Contemporaries." *Bibliographica* 2 (1896):437–51. Research at PRO uncovers facts about London printing career.

Purcell, H. D. "*The Celestina* and the *Interlude of Calisto and Melibea*." *BHS* 44 (1967):1–15. Attempts to determine the relationship *Celestina* and *Calisto*, suggests French redaction as source, calls it an adaptation, praises its compression of time and action, and points out its "English" qualities.

Roberts, R. J. "John Rastell's Inventory of 1538." *Library*, 6th ser., 1 (March 1979):34–42. Raises questions about output.

Rosenbach, A. S. W. "The Influence of *The Celestina* in the Early English Drama." *Jahrbuch der deutschen Shakespeare-Gesellschaft* 39

(1903):43–61. Argues *Calisto*'s brevity improves staging, makes characters more forceful, and brings themes into focus.

Willoughby, Edwin Eliott. "Printer's Mark of John Rastell." *Library Quarterly* 6 (1936):420–21. Discusses second printing emblem.

4. Dissertation

Pacholski, Richard Allen. "The Humanist Drama of the Sir Thomas More Circle." Ph.D. dissertation, University of Wisconsin, 1969. Disagrees with Hogrefe's and Bevington's interpretations, examines five interludes, and modifies critical commonplaces about such drama being "thematically humanistic, theatrically dull, and aesthetically mediocre."

Index

001.3
R229

115 873

DATE DUE

DEMCO 38-297